MANIFESTING GOD

MANIFESTING GOD

THOMAS KEATING

Lantern Books • New York

A Division of Booklight Inc.

2005
Lantern Books
One Union Square West, Suite 201
New York, NY 10003

Scripture quotes are from the *North American Bible,* 1986, 1991, Confraternity of Christian Doctrine, 3211 Fourth St., N.E., Washington, DC 20017

Printed in Canada

Library of Congress Cataloging-in-Publication Data

Keating, Thomas.
  Manifesting God / Thomas Keating.
       p. cm.
  ISBN 1-59056-085-X (alk. paper)
  1. Contemplation. I. Title.
BV5091.C7K4188 2005
248.3'4—dc22

2005018288

With thanks to Bonnie Shimizu, in appreciation for her dedication and hard work on this and other projects.

CONTENTS

FOREWORD

To reject the contemplative dimension of any religion is to reject the religion itself, however loyal one may be to its externals and rituals. This is because the contemplative dimension is the heart and soul of every religion. It initiates the movement into higher states of consciousness.

The great wisdom teachings of the Vedas, Upanishads, Buddhist Sutras, Old and New Testaments, and the Koran—to name a few of the best known—bear witness to this truth.

Right now there are about two billion Christians on the planet. If a significant portion of them were to embrace the contemplative dimension of the Gospel, the emerging global society would experience a powerful surge toward enduring peace. If this contemplative dimension of the Christian religion is not presented, the Gospel is not being adequately preached.

What is the essence of the message that the Christian contemplative tradition seeks to impart? It is the *experience* Jesus had of the Father (Ultimate Reality) as *Abba*. While the sacraments, rituals, doctrines, ascetical practices, ministries, works of mercy, service to others, and prayers of every kind are all oriented to this experience, what Jesus calls "prayer in secret" (see Matthew 6:6) is the most privileged means of accessing it. This practice later became known in the Christian tradition as "contemplation."

Centering Prayer is a contemporary expression of this ancient practice as interpreted by the Fathers and Mothers of the Desert and reported by John Cassian in the fourth century.[1] Cassian transplanted this teaching to the West. In the sixth century, it became enshrined in the Rule of St. Benedict and the monastic orders that sprang from it. In our time it is waiting to be reactivated. It belongs by right not only to monastics but to all Christians in virtue of their common Baptism.

The four Gospels contain Jesus' program for revolutionizing our understanding of the Ultimate Reality and hence of ourselves and other people, and indeed of all created reality. This is the God that is *manifesting* who he is at every moment, in and through us and through all creation. Jesus' teaching initiates us into how to take part in this cosmic adventure. For human beings, it is the most daunting challenge there is—the challenge of becoming fully human. For to become fully human is to become fully divine.

---

1. *Conferences of Cassian* transl. by Colm Luibheid, Classics of Christian Spirituality, Paulist Press, 1985.

CHAPTER ONE

Prayer as Relationship

Every word we say about God has a meaning beyond the one that the word connotes. More precisely, to say "God" is also to say *not* "God." As St. Thomas Aquinas (1225–1274) taught, whatever we say about God is more unlike God than saying nothing. If we do say something, it can only be a pointer toward the Mystery that can never be articulated in words. All that words can do is point in the direction of the Mystery. Even that can be misleading, because we do not normally point to what is already here.

To feel comfortable with the Ultimate Reality whom we call "God" in the Christian tradition is both the reassurance and the challenge that Jesus presented in his teaching. The first thing he said when he began to preach was, "Repent" (Matthew 4:17). This word does not refer to penitential exercises or external practices but means *change the direction in which you are looking for happiness.* Jesus' teaching clearly implies that our present direction does not lead to where happiness can be found, and still less to where God can be found.

The contemplative dimension of the Gospel is Christ's program for getting acquainted with the Ultimate Reality as it really is, which is "no thing." "No thing" means no particular thing, whether concept, feeling or bodily experience. God just *is*—without any limitation. And the way to connect with this "Is-ness" is to just *be*, too.

The problem is that the person who we think we are— that individual full of programs for success, social status, fame, power, affection and esteem, compulsions, addictions, etc.—is not the authentic man or woman that we are. And not only are we *not* who we think we are, but other people are not who we, or they, think they are. Our judgments about our character and other people's characters—and the reality of the world within and around us— are largely incorrect. We see everything upside down or from the perspective of downright ignorance.

The question that perplexes many people at the beginning of this century is: *Who is God?* If this is too abstract a way of posing the question, it can be put it another way: What is your *relationship* with God?

The question of our relationship with God is crucial. There are, of course, as many relationships with God as there are people. The essential point to grasp is that God is very close to us—as open to adults as to the little child who is only able to pray, "Now I lay me down to sleep." While God is pleased with every sincere prayer, God seems to hope that our relationship with him is going to develop so that our prayer is not just a matter of getting through the night, as may be the case with a child, but of living everyday life in God's presence.

St. Thomas Aquinas taught that God is existence and hence is present in everything that exists. If God is present everywhere, it follows that under no circumstances can we ever be separated from him. We may feel that we are; we may think that we are. But in actual fact, there is no way that we can ever be apart from God even if we try. Indeed, God's presence is so present that in some circumstances we may wish that he would take a vacation!

The Story of Job

Such was the case with God's servant Job (cf. Job 1:1–12). In this well-known story, Job is presented as a very wealthy man, highly regarded by his peers, and one who keeps away from all evil. God allows Satan to destroy everything that he owns or holds dear. As his misfortunes multiply, so do his complaints. They might be summarized in these terms: "I've had enough! Turn your eyes away from me and look at somebody else for a change" (cf. Job 7:19).

Job's afflictions under Satan's malign influence increase and he becomes enraged. No one ever accused God of more horrendous crimes than Job. For instance, he unabashedly asserts that God is the murderer of the innocent. We would expect God to say in response, "You miserable little clay man! Who are you to sit in judgment on me?" and then blast him to smithereens! But God doesn't respond to Job right away. He just waits. He listens patiently to all of Job's complaints and accusations.

Eventually Job completely loses his own patience and starts making outrageous demands that might be paraphrased in these words, "I want my day in court! I want to bring the Almighty to justice. He is cruelly punishing me and I've done nothing wrong." Job's fair-weather friends (Eliphaz the Temanite, Bildad the Shuhite, and Zophar the Naamathite—euphemistically called "comforters" [Job 2:11])—keep telling him that he must have committed some terrible sin or he would not have been reduced to these dreadful straits. These cold comforters are sold on the popular theory of their time that suffering is always a punishment for sin. But Job maintains his innocence. He *knows* he is innocent! He is too upright to say that he has done wrong when his conscience bears witness to the fact that he has not.

Job's predicament represents, in a greatly magnified form, the confusion and anger that everyone experiences when trying hard to lead a good life—honoring one's commitments, worshipping God, and showing compassion to others—but experiencing little or no help from God. Instead of enjoying God's favor, all Job's possessions are stolen, his family is destroyed, his reputation is in tatters, and his body is covered with painful sores from head to foot. He is reduced externally and internally to nothing. Job's "friends" are the paradigms of well-intentioned people who try to console those who are going through excruciating suffering by plying them with pious platitudes. They only succeed in making Job feel worse.

Who is this God who, to judge by human standards, treats Job so abominably?

At the end of the story, God speaks to Job out of a whirlwind. God turns out to be not an image or a concept, but an experiential presence. Job doesn't get any explanation for his monumental afflictions, but he gets something far better: the direct *experience* of God. This causes him to withdraw all his complaints. During the course of the lengthy confrontation, God evidently moves Job to a higher state of faith and love. The experience of God as Ultimate Reality, not the pious exhortations of his would be "comforters," heals Job's questioning and emotional turmoil. By means of this encounter with Ultimate Reality Job is fully reconciled with God and with himself. He adjusts his "whys" about the situation—"Why me? Why my family? Why my reputation?"—to the fact that God simply *is*.

God then gives Job twice as much as he had before: land, livestock, wealth, long life, friends, family and good reputation. These are not just material rewards for enduring unimaginable hardships. They are external signs of the spiritual gifts that God pours out upon Job as their friendship moves to divine union.

The Gospel moves beyond Job's encounter with God

and invites us not only to union, but to *intimacy* with God. This is the primary purpose of what Christian theology calls the Incarnation. The God of Christian faith becomes a human being in the person of Jesus and, in doing so, becomes not only one with the human family as a whole, but one with each of its members in particular. In Paul's explanation of this relationship Jesus Christ is the head of the human family in a vastly more real and profound sense than Adam and Eve, who according to the book of Genesis were its physical progenitors.

If Christ, the Eternal Word, became a human being, emerging from the bosom of the Father into material creation, it must mean that Jesus in his human nature knew God in a way that no one else could ever know him. The Godhead dwells in Jesus bodily (Colossians 2:9). Christianity is not so much a series of propositions about God as it is the communication of the intimate *knowledge* that Jesus had of *Who God Is*. The Christian religion is the *transmission* of that experience of Ultimate Reality as *Abba*, Jesus' endearing Aramaic word for Father.

Jesus reveals who God is in ways that we can understand—at least to some degree. For most of Christian history these ways of knowing have not been practiced. Even today, the recognition of the *oneness* of the human family, symbolized by the Creation story and manifested by the Incarnation, is rarely manifested in human affairs. To judge by history, we are basically a highly competitive, self-centered, and violent species. If we accept the research of anthropologists, *Homo sapiens* is barely fifty thousand years old. Give us another fifty thousand years and we might improve. But right now, few actually identify with the human family in such a way that they feel the sufferings and joys of others as their own.

Christ's Experience of *Abba*

The interconnectedness and interdependence of everything that exists is the way the scientific community is beginning to understand material reality. Most of us have yet to be convinced of the reality of this basic structure of the universe. The most effective way to grasp this truth is to experience it. This is one of the precious gifts that the discipline of Contemplative Prayer communicates. It transmits Christ's experience of God as *Abba*. The Aramaic word *Abba* roughly means "daddy"—an affectionate and intimate term of endearment that a child invents for a tenderly loving father. Jesus' experience of God as *Abba* (cf. Mark 14:36) was revolutionary in the cultural context of his time. Jesus' *Abba*, however, is not like any father we know. He is rather the source of everything that is, from the tiniest quark to the largest galaxy.

The word "Father" was occasionally applied to God in the Old Testament by the people of Israel. The God of Israel was worshipped as the God of infinite power, transcendence, majesty, and justice; the author of the Ten Commandments and of innumerable religious and ritual prescriptions. He was the God of armies who had to be worshipped in a special way; a sensitive God who was easily offended; a God to whom one had to atone for failing to observe his laws and rituals; a punishing God who had to be placated by a wide variety of sacrifices and acts of worship, praise, and thanksgiving.

Our Experience of *Abba*

Jesus, on the other hand, teaches that God is closer than we are to ourselves—closer than breathing, closer than thinking, closer than choosing, closer than consciousness itself. In the saying about prayer in the Sermon on the Mount (Matthew 6:6), Jesus teaches that when we pray, we are to pray to *Abba*—not to the God of armies or to the God of strict justice, but to the God who is leaning over us like the most tender of parents. The God proclaimed by Jesus is every human relationship of love that is beautiful, good, and true—all rolled into one and multiplied a trillion times over. According to Jesus' teaching, God's relationship to us is characterized by immense and continuous concern, care and tenderness, and by an all-inclusive forgiveness that extends to everything in our lives, from the moment of our conception until our death.

God's closeness is presupposed in Jesus' wisdom saying about how to pray. The word *Abba* emphasizes a most intimate way of relating to God. According to St. Teresa of Avila, many people pray as if God were absent. Imagine talking to somebody about what one most wants or needs whom you think isn't there! How stupid can you get?!

"When you want to pray," Jesus implies by using the word *Abba*, "speak to someone you believe is not only *there* but listening with loving and rapt attention."

Jesus established this close relationship between the Father and us by taking the whole human family to himself. Through his Incarnation Jesus shared with us his own divine dignity, empowering us with the capacity to be sons and daughters of God. When the apostles ask Jesus to teach them to pray, he teaches them to say, "*Our* Father who art in heaven" (italics mine). St. Paul expresses this special relationship thus:

> For those who are led by the Spirit are children of God. For you did not receive a spirit of slavery to fall back into fear, but you received a spirit of adoption, through which we cry, *Abba*, Father. The Spirit itself bears witness with our spirit that we are children of God, and if children, then heirs and joint heirs with Christ . . . (Romans 8:14–17).

To call God "*our* Father" implies that the experience that Jesus enjoyed has been transmitted to us.

The Nature of God's Closeness

Centering Prayer is patterned on the formula given by Jesus in Matthew 6:6:

> If you want to pray, enter your inner room, close

the door, and pray to your Father in secret, and your Father who sees in secret will reward you.

Entering "your inner room" and "praying to your Father in secret" are obviously aimed at deepening our relationship with God. What happens in the inner room is a process of growing in "the deep knowledge of God" (Colossians 1:11). God of course does not actually come closer; rather God's *actual* closeness at all times and in every place begins to penetrate our ordinary consciousness. To live in the presence of God on a continuous basis can become a kind of fourth dimension to our three-dimensional world, forming an invisible but real background to everything that we do or that happens in our lives.

Most people do not think of God as present all the time, let alone experience that presence. But this is our misfortune. What we take to be our everyday life is full of misconceptions. For example, we humans—all of us—are walking upside down on the planet. It is just gravity that keeps us from wandering off into space. Although in fact we stick out into space head first, nobody feels it, so scientists have to remind us that what we take for granted is not the way things actually are. Time and space as we see them are projections of a brain that seeks order and certitude. Spending regular periods of time in our inner room is a way of recognizing levels of reality beyond the limited dimensions of ordinary awareness.

Why do we find it so hard to believe that God is present at every moment? One possible answer might be that we are not sure we want to be in God's presence all the time. Jesus invites us, urgently, to cultivate that relationship, but we may be more interested in other preoccupations—the childish things that Paul exhorts us to grow out of (1 Corinthians 13:11). Faith is an invitation to grow out of inadequate ways of relating to God into the reality that God actually *is*.

The Christian tradition is the transmission of the relationship with the living God that Jesus experienced. Participation in his own consciousness of God as *Abba* is what Jesus called the Kingdom of God. This kingdom is not a geographical location, an institution, or a form of government. It is a state of consciousness and of enlightened faith. To enter it, the preconceived ideas and prepackaged values that we brought with us from early childhood have to be re-evaluated and outgrown.

CHAPTER TWO

The Parable of the Great Banquet

The parables of the Gospel are stories that reveal the nature of God as Jesus knew him. A significant part of Jesus' wisdom teaching is in them. He repeats that teaching explicitly elsewhere in his teaching. Still, the arresting quality of the parables awakens insights that ordinary speech may not do. That is why a good story sometimes works more effectively in our consciousness than great eloquence; that's why we like novels, movies, and plays. Some stories touch on truths that we rarely reflect on in the ordinary give and take of everyday life.

Let us look at what two parables in particular reveal about the nature of God as *Abba*. First, the parable in Luke's Gospel about the great banquet (Luke 14:16–23).[2]

In order to understand this parable it is necessary to grasp the context in which it was given. For Jesus' hearers the term "great banquet" was loaded. It called to mind

---

2. Matthew allegorizes the parable for his pastoral purposes and in so doing shifts the meaning and basic thrust of the original intent of Jesus.

the popular myth foretold by the Prophets regarding the triumph of Israel over its enemies. The Israel of the first century of the common era had long been under the heavy boot of the Roman Empire. The social, political and religious autonomy of the people had been suppressed for decades. The Messianic myth was based on the expectation that God would destroy the enemies of Israel, after which all the nations of the world would become part of the theocratic kingdom of Israel. God's victory would then be celebrated with a great banquet on top of a mountain.

The social structure of the culture of Palestine at the time was strictly stratified according to social status. You belonged to the class into which you were born and could not rise out of it, similar to the way the "untouchables" are treated in India to this day. Social systems have always been a favorite way for those in power to maintain their control. These systems of stratification may be ethnic, nationalistic, or religious. Jesus' teaching in the parables is that in God's eyes there are no social boundaries. Jesus continually emphasizes by his teaching and example the truth of the basic unity and equality of all the members of the human family.

The writer of the Gospel whom we know as Matthew was writing for the Jewish population who never mentioned out loud the sacred name of God revealed to Moses (Exodus 3:14). Jesus not only mentions God's name out loud, but translates the word "Father" with the endearing term, *Abba*. Thus, in one fell swoop, the unmentionable name becomes not just Father, but the intimate term for father within a particular family. In so doing, Jesus cuts through legalism and the presupposition of distance from God and replaces them with the proclamation of a close, caring, protecting, tender, forgiving, and healing relationship between God and us.

In the parable of the great banquet Jesus undercuts the popular belief in the Messianic Banquet that was firmly embedded in the minds of the people who were listening to him. Even Jesus' disciples couldn't grasp Jesus' idea of the Kingdom until after his resurrection. In this parable, Jesus not only breaks down all barriers to a relationship with God, but dissolves the social barriers of everyday life and tells us that *everyone*—rich or poor, mentally or physically able or disabled—is invited to divine union:

> First of all, then, I ask that supplications, prayers, petitions, and thanksgiving be offered for everyone . . . who wills everyone to be saved and come to the knowledge of the truth (1Timothy 2:1, 4).

The householder is one of the elite of a small town. Only the elite lived in houses—the best the poor could hope for was a roof over their heads. There were only two social classes in Palestinian villages—the very rich and the very poor. The householder prepares a banquet and invites his peers, who are other landowners belonging to his stratum of society.

The first people the host was likely to invite would, of course, be his distinguished peers. In the world of Jesus' time the elite experienced their self-worth through the honor they received from their peers. One of these honors would have been attendance at important celebrations such as one of the elite might put on. However, as the parable relates, the first three distinguished persons whom the householder invites decline with rather lame excuses. Each excuse—property to look after, cattle to test, recent marriage—emphasizes the sense of rejection that this man increasingly experienced. Ignored by his peers, there is no place for him to go on the social ladder but down. He has become, through no fault of his own, an outcast from the community of the elite.

According to the parable, the householder flies into a rage. The dinner is ready but those invited will not come. He tells his servants, "Go out into the highways and byways and bring in the blind, the lame, the halt, the maimed and the poor, so that my house may be filled." The servants rush out and collect a crowd of disabled and underprivileged folk but the banquet is not filled.

The prophets of Israel had taught that the poor were the apple of God's eye. The hero of the Psalms is, in fact, anyone afflicted for God's sake, not just destitute of material goods. It was thus no surprise to the hearers of the parable when the poor and afflicted were invited to attend the great banquet.

However, the arrival of the poor and physically disabled does not fill the banquet hall. The householder is faced with a dilemma. He has lost his honor with his peers and is now faced with the option of either calling off the banquet or inviting more people. He decides on the latter and orders his servants: "Go out into the highways and hedgerows and make the people come in, that my house may be filled" (Luke 14:23). In other words, "Pick up everybody that you find on the street or hiding under a bridge, and drag them in so that my house may be filled." Or to be more specific, bring in the tax collectors, public sinners, prostitutes, the marginalized, the people nobody wants.

At last the banquet hall is filled. One can imagine the general makeup of the crowd. Most of them are in rags, unwashed, destitute, ill at ease, and with very little interest in the householder or the purpose of the banquet. The householder now has to make a critical decision. He can call off the banquet, or he can further humble himself and throw away the last vestige of his honor by sitting down to the meal with these disreputable people.

In the culture of first century Palestine, sharing a meal was the sign of *identification* with those at table. Thus, if the householder joins in the meal, he is identifying himself with the marginalized, the no-gooders, and public sinners. That is why the religious authorities and even the disciples of John the Baptist were so horrified when Jesus ate with tax collectors and prostitutes. The fact that the parable makes clear up to this point is that *everyone*, no matter who they are, is invited to the banquet; and not only invited, but in some cases, *forced* to come in.

The parable now reveals its extraordinary message. The householder—symbol as we saw of God the Father—has lost his honor and status as a member of the socially elite of this town and now is faced with the further humiliation of identifying himself with the dregs of society. Instead of calling off the feast, the householder chooses to throw away the last vestige of his honor and *joins*, not only the poor and afflicted, but the public sinners and rejects of society. *He completely joins them!* This is what God actually does in the Incarnation of his Beloved Son. In completely identifying with sinners, God becomes the opposite of who he is by divine right and dignity. God becomes a human being just where human beings are, sinners in desperate need of forgiveness and healing. Evidently God wills, at any cost, to communicate his inner life to us. The parable thus lifts a corner of the veil that hides who God is.

This parable suggests some other profoundly arresting aspects of the God whom Jesus knows as *Abba*. God seems to prefer *not* to be God in order to manifest the utterly non-possessive attitude that the Trinitarian relationships have to the divine riches, honor, and power. The parable subtly hints at how the three persons of the Trinity relate: the Father, who initially enjoys the fullness of the Godhead, empties himself into the Son in such a way that the Son becomes consubstantial with the Father.

This means that the Son is everything that the Father is except for the Father's relationship to the Godhead as source of the divine relationships. The Father enjoys the Godhead to share and give away, and the Son to receive and to return all to the Father. Together they rejoice in the infinite goodness of the Godhead in their eternal act of total surrender of that glory to each other.

The person of the Holy Spirit is the expression of their infinite joy and bliss. Perhaps we could say that the Holy Spirit continuously reconstitutes the Father and the Son as they eternally give themselves away to each other. All three relationships live in each other rather than in themselves.

The parable in a special way sheds a powerful light on the dynamics of the Word made Flesh. Christ, the Son of God, becomes effectively the slave of the human family and not just a member of the fallen human race. He takes upon himself all the psychological stress and pain of marginalized people, their rejection by society, the burden of their guilty consciences, and their sense of abandonment by God. This divine humility is a disposition that is hard for us to comprehend—a love that intends to incorporate the very dregs of humanity into the Kingdom of God. In short, it does not matter who we are—we are still invited to the banquet. Thus the whole of the Kingdom is ours for the *accepting*.

One of the issues that Jesus addresses in the parable is the assumption that God is someone whose favor we must earn. In fact, the idea that we have to behave in a certain way to win his love risks missing the sheer gratuity of the gift and thus missing the invitation. The problem with the elite in any society is that they do not realize the dangerous condition they are in. Status, power, and wealth tend to hide from them the truth about themselves. Until they have been through such trauma as a painful divorce, serious illness, bankruptcy proceedings, or loss of loved ones, reputation, or social status like Job did, they do not know who they are. The elite not infrequently have to be confronted by enormous tragedy in order to grasp the emptiness and inadequacy of their own ideas of happiness as well as the full extent of God's love for them.

CHAPTER THREE

The Parable of the Leaven

The parable of the leaven reinforces this teaching. It goes like this: "The Kingdom of God is like leaven which a woman took and hid in three measures of flour till it was all leavened" (Luke 13:20–21).

When the Israelites celebrated the feast of the Passover, they were forbidden to use leavened bread. It could not even be kept in one's house during Passover. Leaven in their society was a symbol of moral corruption. Leaven was made by placing a piece of bread in a dark damp place until it began to decay and stink. Leavened bread was thus a lively symbol of the unholy and the profane— in short, everyday life.

Jesus' comparison of the Kingdom of God to leaven must have astonished his hearers.

The amount of dough that the woman in the parable used—which was considerable—is the precise measure that Abraham's wife Sarah provided for the three angels at the oaks of Mamre when God visited Abraham

(Genesis 18). That incident had come to be recognized in the popular mind as an epiphany of God's presence. Thus, for those listening, Jesus was not only identifying the Kingdom of God with leaven, the symbol of moral corruption, but implying, by mentioning so large an amount of dough, that the Kingdom is like *monumental* moral corruption.[3]

After this brief parable, Jesus walks off down the street. There is no explanation, no answer to the questions flooding the stunned minds of the hearers, one of which must have been, "Is this man saying that moral evil is good?"

Of course, the parable also challenges our ideas of what is good and what is evil. It is as if Jesus says to us, "What makes you so sure?" Job experienced God as acting unjustly in his overwhelming trials. He did not know what to make of such ill treatment because for him God was the infinitely Just One who faithfully rewards good and punishes evil.

The parable of the leaven also implies that what we think is the worst thing that could happen to us may actually be the coming of the Kingdom of God into our lives. Or, to put it differently, the Kingdom is most powerful where we least expect to find it and where we may not even want to find it.

We bring with us from early childhood various ideas of God that we absorbed unquestioningly from parents and

---

3. For more about this view of the Parable of the Leaven cf. *St. Thérèse of Lisieux*, Thomas Keating (Lantern Books, 2001), pp. 21–37.

teachers during the socialization period from roughly four to eight years of age. Though I have touched on some of these ideas before, let me recapitulate them here for the purposes of grasping the full implications of this parable:

1. God dwells in inaccessible light.
2. God is infinitely just and rewards the good and relentlessly punishes evildoers.
3. God protects us if we faithfully pray and observe all his commandments.
4. We have to placate God for our sins by penitential acts.
5. God requires us to deny ourselves every pleasure in order to win his favor.

These attitudes have a certain basis in truth, but they also have serious limitations. The Christian path is not about defining God, but of enlarging our *idea* of God. Even with the help of doctrine, rituals, good deeds, and moral certainties, without the experience of God's mercy and forgiveness, we do not really know who God is.

We have to learn to think *big* of God! He is not rigid, narrow-minded, fussy, or hard to please, but, as the Psalmist proclaims, God is "slow to anger and rich in mercy" (Psalm 103:8). "His steadfast love endures forever" (Psalm 136).

Jesus in the parable undercuts the facile conviction that we know with certitude what moral good and evil actually are. This certitude renders us incapable of finding God in what, in our view, is moral evil.

Besides moral corruption, there are of course, other forms of evil that afflict us, such as physical illness, natural disasters, and the loss of loved ones, possessions, or reputation. We also tend to perceive emotional, mental or spiritual problems as evil. For example, the ups and downs of the spiritual journey contain alternating periods of consolation and desolation. The latter is often perceived as an unmitigated evil. Actually, something that we do not want to happen may actually be the best thing that could possibly happen to us.

God usually sends us what we need, not what we want or think we need, and still less what we deserve. That is because God is so close and knows us so intimately that he already is well aware of what we need, so wise that he never makes a mistake, and so compassionate that he is ever ready to forgive and forget. Hence, we would be naïve to exclude God from any situation that arises in our lives. A tragedy or disaster may be the only set of circumstances that can move us beyond our prepackaged values and preconceived ideas to a deeper level of relating to God in trust, self-surrender, and love.

The Parable of the Publican and the Pharisee

In the parable of the publican and the pharisee (Luke 18:10–14), it is not the holy place that provides salvation, but in everyday life. The publican briefly acknowledges himself as a public sinner and asks for God's mercy. He goes home to his house "justified"—that is, ready to meet daily life with a right relationship with God. The pharisee, on the other hand, thanks God for his good deeds and is completely oblivious to the fact that his religious status and the holy place in which he is praying are not doing him the good that he takes for granted. The parable affirms that it is not the *place*, however holy, where the Kingdom of God is most active; nor is it our religious *status*. It is present rather in an *attitude* of complete honesty toward God, other people, and ourselves. This is what humility is. Through Contemplative Prayer—through staying in our inner room—we become willing to let go of our illusion that the way we see the world is the right way or what is worse, the only way. It isn't.

Attachment to our roles in life hinders us actually fulfilling them. Once we are finally willing to let go of our roles, we may receive them back, like Job, with twice as much as we had before, at least from a spiritual perspective. If some significant wake-up call does not happen, we may never face the fact that we are locked into a role or a relationship with someone or something that we are not willing to relinquish for the love of God. With those dispositions, God cannot transmit to us the fullness of the Kingdom.

In the parable of the leaven, Jesus teaches clearly that the Kingdom is more active in us than we ever dared dream of. Normally, we would just as soon postpone difficulties or disappointments until next week or preferably next month. God, however, is sometimes not inclined to wait, but says *"now."* In the indignities and sufferings that we may experience, what is most painful is not what happens, but our *attitude* to what happens. This is why when we pray for deliverance from evil, God often does not take away our difficulties, but *joins* us in enduring them. That is a greater gift than taking away the trial. It is a much greater gift because it unites us to the cross of Christ and to his redemptive activity. Through our union with him, we are sharing in the greatest project in human life, which is the redemption of the world. To suffer in union with Christ is to offer to those we love and try to serve the greatest of all gifts, the one that we have been freely given: God's unconditional love.

One of God's characteristics revealed in Scripture that is most lovable is tenderness (cf. Hosea 11:8). This is an aspect of the Divine Feminine, which translates in our awareness of God as motherly, affectionate, nurturing, patient, forgiving, reconciling opposites, healing every wound, innocence itself.

God is innocence itself. Like a happy child, God seems to have no particular agenda, just sheer goodness manifesting itself. God is eternally childlike and playful, accepting everything just as it is. God is always in the present moment with whatever may be its contents: always responding to everything and everyone; yet always free, peaceful, and at rest. God delights in everything that exists, adjusting to every creature (personal with creatures that are persons, impersonal with creatures that are impersonal) and eager to bestow eternal life and happiness on every human being.

CHAPTER FOUR

Forgiveness

Forgiveness is central to the Christian religion. It was Jesus' chief concern on the night of his resurrection when he revealed himself to the Apostles gathered together behind locked doors, breathed on them, and said, "Receive the Holy Spirit. Whose sins you forgive are forgiven them. Whose sins you retain are retained" (John: 20:22–23). These words are normally understood to refer to the Sacrament of Reconciliation in the Roman Catholic communion. They may also have a further significance.

The Father is nothing but forgiveness. We too must practice forgiveness to be God's children. There may be events and people in our conscious and unconscious memories that we have not forgiven. This leaves them in deep, even if repressed, psychological pain. It is in our power to heal them or to leave them in their pain.

The true self in us—the Divine Indwelling—wants to forgive, but is overlain by layers of the false self that keeps the disposition of unforgiveness in place. In actual fact, not to forgive others is not to forgive ourselves. At the deepest level we are everyone else. We can only enjoy the world of unconditional love with hearts that are completely open to everyone.

Shame, guilt, and despair; tormenting desires of lust, gluttony, greed and pride; dark emotions of envy, hatred, indifference to others' desperate needs—these are the kinds of negative emotions that were in the cup that Jesus prayed to be delivered from in the Garden of Gethsamane. The blows of his physical scourging and crown of thorns manifested outwardly the psychological and spiritual suffering that was inwardly tearing him apart. Our unjust attitudes, unwillingness to forgive, and fully deliberate sins are the true cause of Jesus' passion and death, certainly not a few Jewish and Roman authorities. Jesus seeks to heal our enormous self-centeredness through his identification with the painful feelings that flow as inevitable consequences from our uneasy consciences, especially when we cannot or will not forgive. Forgiveness includes the harm we have suffered from institutions as well as from people.

If we are offenders and are not forgiven, there is always something missing in our lives. Even if we have done what we could to be reconciled with another person and the other will not respond or accept our apology, we may be at peace because we did what we could, but something will still be missing. There may be enormous pain if the other was formerly very dear and very close to us.

Forgiveness is only complete when *both* persons forgive each other. This is what reconciliation is. It is the triumph of Christ's passion, death and resurrection. Reconciliation is the central theme of the Gospel.

We must above all forgive God for what we do not like in ourselves and in our lives. The experience of God's forgiveness heals our wounds and enables us to forgive ourselves even if others refuse to forgive us. This is an enormous boost to confidence in God and in our true selves.

How can we know if we have been forgiven by God? By fully forgiving others. In this way we know with certainty that God has forgiven us and thus we can finally forgive ourselves.

In Christ's death, *That Which Is* becomes that which is not. God cannot of course die, but God can die in us. The Son became one of us in order to manifest who the Father is. In some way, God dies in Jesus' death. The Eternal Word of God becomes silent. All that the Father is— Godself—is battered, crucified, and destroyed in Jesus, its human form. The love that is beyond love, however, remains: Infinite Love sacrificing itself out of Infinite Love.

What remains when the Son gives up Infinite Love for the Father by becoming sin? That is the Ultimate Reality whom we call God in the Christian religion: love beyond love beyond love.

CHAPTER FIVE

The Most Excellent Path

The heart of the Christian spiritual journey is God's determined will to transmit to us the maximum of divine light, life, love and happiness that we can possibly receive.

In 1 Corinthians 1:12, Paul describes the charismatic gifts that are given by the Holy Spirit to build up the local Christian community: speaking in tongues, interpretation of tongues, healing, prophecy, working miracles, inspired teaching, inspired preaching, administration, and the word of wisdom. All of these gifts are given to encourage and strengthen the community as a whole; but they do not compare with the gift of the transformation of the roots of our faculties and the substance of our soul, which is the work of sanctifying grace.

A fundamental truth of the Judeo-Christian revelation is that we are made in the image of God. That image is our basic goodness. Nothing on earth, in the next life, or anywhere else can ever change it. It is the source of the immense dignity of every human being. Each person has the innate capacity for divine union.

Paul, having whetted the appetite of his disciples for the spiritual journey in his letter to the Corinthians with a full listing of the charismatic gifts, concludes with this striking statement: "Now I will show you the way that *surpasses all others*" (emphasis added). In other words, no matter how numerous or exalted the charismatic gifts that we may possess, they cannot match the more excellent path of pure love. They cannot compare with the grace of inward transformation through which the divine life itself is actually transmitted to us. Paul writes:

> If I speak with human tongues and angelic as well but do not have love, I am a noisy gong or a clanging cymbal. If I have the gift of prophecy and with full knowledge comprehend all mysteries; if I have faith great enough to move mountains, but have not love, I am nothing. If I give everything I have to feed the poor and hand over my body to be burned, but have not love, I gain nothing.
>
> Love is patient. Love is kind. Love is not jealous. It does not put on airs. It is not snobbish. Love is never rude. It is not self-seeking. It is not prone to anger. Neither does it brood over injuries. Love does not rejoice in what is wrong, but rejoices in the truth. There is no limit to love's forbearance, to

its trust, its hope, its power to endure. Love never fails.

Prophecies will cease, the gift of tongues will be silent, knowledge will pass away. Our knowledge is imperfect and our prophesying is imperfect. When the perfect comes, the imperfect will pass away. Then I shall know even as I am known.

There are in the end three things that last: faith, hope and love, and the greatest of these is love" (1 Corinthians 13).

This detailed description of the way divine love functions in human affairs does not praise sentimentality or the *feeling* of love, but instead presents divine love as the self-giving disposition that in Greek is called *agape* and in Latin *caritas*. This term points to the eternal exchange of unconditional love in the Trinity between the Father, the Son, and the Holy Spirit.

This text is further enhanced by the passage in the First Epistle of John, that states that "God is love" (4:8)—that is to say, God not only *shows* love but *is* love. If, with Paul, we look at the movement of the spiritual journey as growth in love, we may see why he calls this the most excellent path: *it is the assimilation of Christ's experience of the Father as Abba*. This aspect of the Gospel is not just a teaching, but the *transmission* of Christ's *Abba* experience. We might call this teaching "the contemplative dimension of the Gospel." Without it, the Gospel is not fully proclaimed. Contemplation is not the reward of virtue, but a *necessity* in order to practice it. Christian history is the poignant story of how well or poorly each generation of Christians has assimilated Christ's *Abba* experience.

God the Father is, of course, Creator and Sustainer of our being at every level—body, soul and spirit—as well as the source of every other being. The word *Abba* that epitomizes Jesus' experience of the Father adds a tender, nurturing, and compassionate understanding of the Ultimate Reality. It emphasizes what might be called the feminine side of the Ultimate Reality.

God is hidden from us chiefly because we do not know how to love in this way. Centering Prayer—and Contemplative Prayer, to which it leads—is totally in the service of getting in touch with the "deep knowledge" of God, which is Paul's term for contemplation.[4] The Spirit, dwelling in our inmost being, communicates to us at every moment the divine presence that is love. "The love of God is poured forth in our hearts by the Holy Spirit who is given to us" (Romans 5:5).

We are used to thinking of love in different ways. The English word "love" tries to cover a variety of meanings: the love of friendship, erotic love, the filial love of a child for its parents and the love of parents for a child, the love of one's country, and the love of ourselves. Divine love, however, is a fire so intense that no one can be fully

---

4. For more about the history and theory of Centering Prayer see Chapter 15.

exposed to it in this life without turning into a grease spot. God has to veil his presence, make use of various disguises, and hide behind secondary causes lest the intensity of divine love force the soul out of the body. To express this truth in a concrete example, St. Augustine comments that the Eucharist is the milk that God has provided in this life because of our spiritual weakness. It is only in the next life, when we have been prepared by this baby food, so to speak, that we can sink our spiritual faculties into the solid food of the divine essence, beyond which there is no greater delight.

The enjoyment of experiencing God's love is characteristic of the early stages of the spiritual journey. Loving God for the sake of spiritual consolation is gradually purified and transformed into *agape*, unconditional love. Divine love tirelessly gives itself away. It even seems to wish to *throw itself away* in order to manifest the divine urgency to pour out its boundless mercy and goodness upon all creation, especially upon human beings who can respond with gratitude, trust and self-surrender and fully enjoy it.

The Eucharist as the Peak of Mysticism

If you have read some of the classics of romantic literature, there is in them a perception that among great lovers, the passion of love becomes so intense at times that the lovers describe their overwhelming attraction as the desire to "eat each other up." This metaphor illumines the ardent longing of the couple to become one with each other in every possible way, even to the point of *becoming the other*. This depth of human love casts light on the profound meaning of the Eucharist. From this perspective, the Eucharist is the peak of Christian mysticism. When we receive the Eucharist, we are plunged instantaneously into the depths of the Trinity. Through the practice of Contemplative Prayer this explosion of divine energy is gradually unpacked so that, little by little, we can perceive in detail the great gifts we have received in the communication of divine light, life and love conferred upon us in this sacrament.

In the reception of the Eucharist the sheer generosity of God's love recommends itself to us. God literally delivers himself into our hands to be eaten. This is the ultimate vulnerability of God, the ultimate expression of the divine humility that literally is giving itself away to people who, for the most part, have only the remotest idea of the incredible gift they are receiving.

When we consume the consecrated bread and wine, the elements are transformed into our bodies through the natural process of digestion. In receiving the Eucharist, however, something greater takes place according to St. Augustine: *we are consumed by the divine energy and transformed into God*. We are engulfed in an infinite embrace. It is as if the Holy Spirit placed a great big kiss in the center of our being, creating ripples that radiate to every level of our being, body, soul and spirit, and flooding it with the inexhaustible energy of divine light, life and love.

Christ comes to us in the Eucharist, not just for a few minutes while the bread and wine are being consumed; he comes to remain forever. To be more exact, the grace of the Eucharist enables us to recognize Christ as already present within us in his divine nature and increasing the intimacy of his presence every time we receive Holy Communion.

The Eucharist inserts us as living cells into the Mystical Body of Christ. We are what the philosopher and writer Arthur Koestler (1905–1983) called a *holon*, a term for a concept I already touched upon in chapters one and two. The word *holon* comes from the Greek word for "whole" and refers to a self-contained organism or unit that contains within it numerous interrelated parts. Through the gift of the Eucharist we become *holons* within the greater *holon* of Christ's Mystical Body. That means that each of us has within us the whole program of divine transformation. The Spirit of God, like the soul in the body, fills the whole body including every organ, and every cell.

The Spirit dwelling in each cell of the Mystical Body puts at our disposal all the spiritual gifts we need to be transformed into the mind and heart of Christ and into full participation in the Kingdom of God. The Kingdom of God, as we saw, is not a geopolitical institution, nor a physical location. It is *the state of consciousness* that Jesus enjoyed as the Word made flesh. *It is Christ's experience as a human being of the Eternal Father as* Abba.

The word *Abba* that Jesus uses for the Father is a term that implies that God is always close, leaning over us, protecting us from without, guiding us from within, and bringing us, step by step, to the full development of the grace of Baptism, which is further enhanced in the reception of the other sacraments.

The spiritual powers bestowed in Baptism are first and foremost the Divine Indwelling, which is the Trinitarian life going on within us continuously and the radical source of our relationship with God. Along with the Divine Indwelling goes a gift that includes all the resources that we need in order to become one body and one spirit with Christ, a state which Christian contemplative tradition calls the Spiritual Marriage. Baptism is an engagement with Christ and these gifts are a kind of trousseau communicated to us in anticipation of the transforming union.

The gift, rooted in the Divine Indwelling, consists of the three Theological Virtues (faith, hope and charity); the four infused Moral Virtues (justice, prudence, temperance, and fortitude); the Fruits of the Spirit that Paul enumerates in Galatians 5:22–23 (charity, joy, peace, meekness, gentleness, self-control, patience, goodness, and faithfulness); and the Seven Gifts of the Holy Spirit (wisdom, understanding, counsel, knowledge, fortitude, reverence, piety) enumerated in Isaiah 11:2, which lead to the Beatitudes. The exercise of these precious treasures and their manifestation in everyday life are signs that Christ is truly risen in us, manifesting the grace of the Resurrection in all our activities, even in the most insignificant. In other words, these treasures are the positive manifestation of the grace we received in Baptism, unfolding within us in a great variety of concrete actions. They enable us to assimilate the mind and heart of Christ and to be assimilated by it.

The supernatural organism and all its aspects grow in us at the same time. Growth in one is growth in all of them. Charity is the core and motive of every genuine virtue, the Fruits of the Spirit, and the beatitudes. It is the most transforming of God's gifts. It awakens the image of God in us, empowering us to manifest the beauty, goodness, and love of the Father in all our thoughts, words, and actions.

What holds us back from activating the gifts of the Holy Spirit is the false self. The false self is the cause of spiritual retardation; it conceals the fundamental experience of being created in the image and likeness of God.

CHAPTER SIX

"Jews" and "Greeks" as Metaphors of Spiritual Progress

The sheer gratuity of God's love invites every human being to participate in Christ's experience of *Abba*, the God who is love.

Saint Paul believed that as we progress in the spiritual journey, we are continuously being transformed.

> All of us, gazing with unveiled face on the glory of the Lord, are being transformed into the same image from glory to glory, as from the Lord who is the Spirit (2 Corinthians 3:18).

We are not the same as we were when we began. Some of the ascetical tools we may have used with good effect to support our spiritual journey in the beginning, or experiences that we counted on to sustain our progress, will no longer be appropriate, or at the very best, will need to be modified, reduced, or dropped.

Paul uses the words "Greeks" and "Jews" as metaphors for those who are progressing in the spiritual journey. Although they may have made real progress, they are now called to move farther along the path and take upon themselves what he calls *the most excellent way*. Paul writes:

> Jews demand signs and Greeks look for wisdom, but we preach Christ crucified: a stumbling block to the Jews and absurdity to the Gentiles; but to those who are called, Jews and Greeks alike, Christ, who is the power of God and the wisdom of God. For God's folly is wiser than men and his weakness more powerful than men (1 Corinthians 1:22–25).

When he writes of "signs," Paul is presumably thinking of spiritual consolations, miracles, charismatic gifts, concrete and prompt answers to our prayers, and coincidences that reassure us of God's closeness or special protection. Paul wants us to realize that as we advance in faith, the time to expect signs and spiritual consolations will pass. He is poking fun at the "Jews" not as a people, but as a symbol of those who think they are serving God greatly and deserve the admiration and thanks of those they are serving. Such aspirations are not wrong; they are just not appropriate or realistic. They show a lack of the purity of love that "the most excellent way" presupposes.

While it is true that Jesus worked all kinds of miracles during his ministry, one senses that he rather regretted this necessity. Fundamentally, signs and miraculous events are designed to strengthen weak faith. Once faith is well established, it doesn't need signs anymore—or, at least, not as frequently. One's faith is based on a growing confidence in God without human props or consoling feelings to support our weakness.

In several places in the Gospel Jesus congratulates people for their degree of advanced faith. The Canaanite woman perseveres in faith even in the presence of Jesus' seeming indifference to her request. In the end, he joyfully proclaims, "Oh woman, great is your faith!" As if to say, "You can have anything you want!"[5]

We also read about a royal official whose son is sick at home (John 4:48–50). The man pleads with Jesus to come and heal the boy, who is near death. Jesus answers, "Unless you see signs and wonders, you will not believe."

The royal official presses his cause, saying, "Sir, come down before my child dies!"

Jesus declines to go but assures the man, "Your son will live."

---

5. See Matthew 15:28.

On the way home, the official learns that his son was cured at the same moment that Jesus said he that would live.

These incidents indicate that Jesus provides signs and works miracles with a certain reluctance. On another occasion he says explicitly:

> An evil and unfaithful generation seeks a sign, but no sign will be given it except the sign of Jonah the prophet. Just as Jonah was in the belly of the whale three days and three nights, so will the Son of Man be in the heart of the earth three days and three nights (Matthew 12:39–40).

Jesus is referring, of course, to the Paschal Mystery, the events that encompass Jesus' passion, death, and resurrection. That is the only sign we need if we are progressing in faith. The divine plan of salvation reserves the reassurance of signs and wonders for people of little faith. The Paschal Mystery is the ultimate sign that sustains those whose faith is maturing. They need nothing more.

Our false self develops a world-view of our own inventing. The pillars on which it rests are two: the emotional programs for happiness based on the instinctual needs of survival and security, affection and esteem, and power and control—and over-identification with the group to which we belong, whether this be ethnicity, tribe, family, nation, religion, peer group, or gang. Our unwillingness to let go of the support systems that keep our false selves in place is the source of every sin. When circumstances challenge our faith, some people fall apart and start lamenting: "Why does God treat me this way?" And the disturbing question that plagues all believers of whatever religion begins to arise, namely, "If God is sovereign over all things, and I keep serving him as best I can, why doesn't he answer my prayers and take away my endless problems and difficulties? What kind of God is this?"

These are the people who need "signs and wonders" to shore up their faith. At some point, however, they will be challenged to grow into a mature faith that does not rely on human props, but on God alone.

The Call to Grow in Trust

In the New Testament, "faith" usually translates best as "trust." Confidence in God reduces the need for signs and wonders. Signs and wonders may still occur—perhaps more often than before. What God asks us to give up is our *attachment* to signs and wonders—both of a miraculous kind and in the form of spiritual consolations. We cannot see God as he is in this world. We have to learn to live contentedly on this side of vision, the side of pure faith that only sees "indistinctly, as in a mirror" (1 Corinthians 13:12). That does not mean that God is not present. It is just that he is not present for the gratification of our instinctual needs and the emotional programs for happiness based on them, now transferred to the experience of the spiritual journey. While we no longer look for happiness in material goods or by climbing the corporate or ecclesiastical ladders, we are still programmed for self-satisfaction in the symbols of self-gratification that the new environment may provide.

In God's relationship with us, there are never any acts of punishment. "God is love" (1 John 4:16). How could infinite love be interested in punishment? We tend to project onto God what we expect authority figures to do if we misbehave or do not keep their laws.

But God isn't this way. What we interpret as punishment, such as failures on God's part to make sure that we never suffer misfortune, are moments of grace designed to heal the wounds of the human condition. Misfortune is a not a sign that God has withdrawn his love from us, but rather that God is calling us to a greater detachment from ourselves and perhaps a greater contribution in the transformation of others.

To put this issue in a different way, what we interpret as difficulties or even disasters are often God's mercy confronting us in ways that are necessary because of our attachments to our emotional programs for happiness and to *how* we expect God to help us. We may even try to dictate to God how we are to be treated. This is clearly not the fruit of pure love. It is rather the exercise of a self-centered love for ourselves that is looking for liberation from all our problems and for ample rewards for our good deeds. If God doesn't measure up to our standards in these areas, we are tempted to withdraw or reduce our service.

This wisdom saying of Paul emphasizes a number of important points. As we saw, the "Jews" represent you and me as we progress in the spiritual journey and start groaning because the former supports that we relied on are being taken away. We want to enjoy consolations in prayer. The "Greeks" at this level of spiritual development seek "wisdom." Paul uses "wisdom" in the sense that the Greek philosophers understood it: as the intellectual vision of truth whereby one passes beyond the usual ups and downs of everyday life and enters into a permanent state of equanimity. I am not referring to oppression, destitution, and other forms of terrible injustice, but to the naïve wish to be free of all difficulties that afflicts those who feel put down by the ordinary circumstances of life. They may have suffered disappointments like financial difficulties, marriage problems, loss of a loved one, addictions, getting old, having to die—all things that are a part of the normal course of life. Jesus' teaching that God's pervasive presence is in everything that happens is unintelligible to them. They perceive only negativity and pain in their various difficulties and disappointments, not the transformation that is occurring.

Living the Parable of the Leaven

In this connection, the parable in which Jesus compares the Kingdom to leaven is worth recalling (Luke 13:20–21). In Jesus' time, as we saw, leaven was a symbol of moral corruption. In that religious atmosphere the sacred was identified with feast days, sacred places and sacred persons. Jesus in this parable is saying, not so. The Kingdom is not limited to rituals and feast days. Where is it, then? According to the parable, it is present and active in the ordinary, the profane, and everyday life.

Thus Jesus revolutionizes the popular idea of the sacred. The Kingdom of God is where you least think it is and where you don't expect to find it. The Kingdom is probably most active where you don't even want to find it! To follow Christ into the Kingdom, we have to give up the myth of rising to some kind of serenity in which nothing can disturb us, or to a wisdom by means of which we can answer all questions and doubts. Indeed, we may find ourselves struggling with monumental corruption within ourselves.

The parable of the leaven can be lived in a cloister. It can be lived on the street, in a private home, a hospital or a place of work. It can be lived on a mountain, in the desert, in a ghetto, on the battlefield, anywhere. If you accept the God of everyday life, you can enjoy God right now in the present moment. If you are looking for a God who is going to rescue you from the problems and difficulties of everyday life, you may have a long wait.

True Nature of the Kingdom of God

The Israelites of Jesus' time, as we saw, were trained to think of God as transcendent and unapproachable. He was the God who would some day deliver Israel from the oppression of the Romans. Their expectations of the Kingdom of God led them to believe that all the nations of the world would accept one day the dominion of Israel. The Messiah to come was definitely a political figure.

The parable of the leaven says: no chance. The coming of the Kingdom is not a success story. On the contrary, the Kingdom is at work in the ordinary circumstances of daily life and is even more active and powerful in difficult situations. Difficulties when accepted for God's sake tend to accelerate the spiritual journey and to move it beyond the routines of selfishness that are so deeply rooted in us.

In Jesus' teaching God is so close and so present that you don't have to go anywhere to find him. You can go on a pilgrimage if you want, and receive great graces along the way; but you don't *have* to go anywhere. There is no special place to go to find God and no place not to go—because he is already *here*, that is, living within us and present in the particular circumstances of the present moment as well as in our reactions to them.

It is *we* who may need to stop going places both mentally or physically. Through the practice of contemplation, we can access the mystery of God's presence within us and manifest the power of grace in the practice of unselfish love. This is the "most excellent way" that Paul recommends. It is a stumbling block to one set of practitioners who haven't gotten beyond the need for signs and wonders. It is folly to those who seek spiritual consolations or simply proof that they are on the right path to divine union. On the contrary, when you do not know where you are going; when you have no proof that you are on the right road; when you are thoroughly confused; when everybody rejects you and speaks ill of you, rejoice! Because this is the shortcut to divine wisdom and participation in the Kingdom. Divine wisdom communicates God's view of reality and opens our eyes to the fact that the Kingdom is most accessible in the ordinary routines and difficulties of everyday life and in the most unacceptable (to us) situations.

CHAPTER SEVEN

Dancing with God

In the previous chapter we discussed the situation of people progressing in the spiritual journey and who experience the withdrawal of the human props they had previously relied on. This experience of "withdrawal" may take an acute form at times. For instance, we may find that our reception of the sacraments, participation in rituals, practice of virtue, reading of Scripture, and the ministry to which we are committed have all gone dry or dead, leaving us with no sense of satisfaction and sometimes with the conviction of utter failure.

In such times we need to be reminded that God is urging and encouraging us to work at the level of pure faith beyond both sense and spiritual experiences. As faith is purified, practices such as rituals, prayer formulas, and spiritual reading, which are excellent in themselves and necessary in the beginning, are often of little or no help.

Such severely tried souls still perform their religious duties, but without any satisfaction. As they persevere, however, they let go of their naïve expectations for the spiritual journey. The experience of their weakness and the disintegration of their support systems are self-evident. They no longer entertain grandiose ideas of the heavens opening and Christ appearing at the right hand of the Father, thanking them for their extraordinary efforts on behalf of the Kingdom. In fact, it almost feels as if God couldn't care less what they do. Here is where the hymn of Paul to divine love is particularly useful: "Love bears everything" (1 Corinthians 13:7). Augustine's paraphrase for this injunction is, "Love bears the unbearable." In other words, love remains calm and peaceful at a deep level even when all of the rest of our faculties are buried in the debris of unfulfilled expectations.

This does not mean, of course, that God does not want us to cultivate a great vision for our lives, but the greatness will not come in the form of the glorification of our egos. Rather, the goal is the glorification of God working in our human weakness. The process alerts us to the fact that an immense and indeed infinite Intelligence is working within us and often in spite of us. While respecting our freedom, God finds ways to bring us around to what God wants us to do, even, at times, against our will. This immense Intelligence reveals itself as an all-embracing and practical love that is far more substantial than signs and wonders. Our expectations of moral perfection, spiritual consolation, and experiences of an ecstatic quality, are gradually shredded. These benefits may be a necessary phase of the spiritual journey for beginners or for those along the way, but the heart of the journey is not rooted in such experiences. Rather, it is rooted in the transformation of our spiritual faculties, attitudes, and motivation, and the growing conviction of God's closeness in all our activities, even the most profane and inconsequential. Is that a surprise? If God made atoms, microbes, and quarks and knows every bird falling to the ground, what is so surprising in God's taking a lively interest in us as his beloved children and friends?

The Divine Dance

How to characterize our relationship from this point on in the spiritual journey with the God who is so close but whose presence is hidden from us? The Christian tradition calls this the life of faith. It is a relationship in which our trust in God is not based on human props or spiritual consolations, but on boundless confidence in God's infinite mercy, forgiveness, and hidden protection. We take refuge in the Father, Son, and Holy Spirit and in Christ Jesus dying and rising again.

As love increases, one feels at times that one is an instrument of God. Maybe it is too personal an experience to generalize, but I have seen it happen in a number of people. If they have certain spiritual gifts, it feels as if someone else is supplying them with the inspiration and energy they need to exercise them.

Such a person might be compared to a pencil that is

picked up at the appropriate time. If that person is inspired to write or speak, he or she knows that the divine Spirit is working through him or her. It is not the same kind of inspiration that we attribute to the authors of Scripture, of course. But these people know that the energy they have is not coming from themselves. When the divine Mover puts down the pencil, their source of energy goes too, and they feel to the full their normal inability to do anything useful for the Kingdom of God . . . until this dynamic presence picks them up again.

The occasions where this happens are as various as life's circumstances. I include among them any ministry—parenting, service to others, and justice and peace issues. All of these things are great concerns of God according to the prophets of the Old and New Testaments. Moreover, there seems to be a divine way of doing everything: a divine way to be a lawyer, doctor, grandmother, teacher, convict, homeless person, or just to be sick. Since the Kingdom of God is present in ordinary circumstances, sensitivity to the movements of the Spirit within us tends to increase. On such occasions, everyday life can become a kind of dance.

If you have ever seen a couple who are superb ballroom dancers, you will recall that their steps are in complete synchronicity. They twirl and turn and stop and start—always at the same time. Their bodies are so closely interwoven you would think they were pieces of a jigsaw puzzle interlocked with each other. Divine Love is our dance partner and invites us to respond in the details of everyday life as to the movements of a dance. Everything one does—walking, sitting, breathing, speaking, working, playing, eating, sleeping—is manifesting the dance. Together with God we co-create the dance. The Creator remains the leader and sets the time, place and pace for each movement that he wants to share with us.

The dance with God is a way to put Paul's hymn to divine love into practice. Recall Paul's words, "Love is kind. Love is not jealous. It does not put on airs. It is not snobbish. Love is never rude. . . . There is no limit to love's forbearance" (1 Corinthians 13). You can intuit from this text how the Divine Partner is leading you. Every action seems to be perfectly choreographed. Others may not notice the dance at all because it is so ordinary. It is so congruent with the way things are supposed to be that it can completely escape notice, unless there is someone there with the eyes of faith to perceive what is going on.

CHAPTER EIGHT

The Divine Indwelling

The skillful expression of our dance with Divine Love is rooted in the practice of Contemplative Prayer. Contemplative Prayer in turn is rooted in the grace of Baptism. It is the growth of the faith received in Baptism. The doctrine of the Divine Indwelling affirms that the Trinity (Father, Son and Holy Spirit) is present in us all the time—morning, noon, and night—and present everywhere else in the universe in virtue of the fact that other things exist. Wherever anything is, God who is "Is-ness" must be present; otherwise, there is nothing to hold any particular expression of "Is-ness" in existence.

Through the regular practice of Contemplative Prayer, faith keeps growing. The sense of the divine presence becomes a kind of second nature or fourth dimension to the time/space continuum. It also manifests itself in everyone else and in every creature. What is important about us is not *us*, therefore, but the *divine presence* in us; in other words, God in us relating to God in everything else.

Our perspective on reality needs to be sensitized to the divine presence so that we can take part appropriately and continuously in the divine dance. The Divine Indwelling relates us to God as the most dynamic of partners. It presupposes that we are willing to respond to the movements of the Spirit within us.

The Divine Spirit guides our body, soul and spirit through the intricate steps that the divine action may wish to take. God doesn't look for an audience or applause. He simply enjoys the dance with each of us. There is a playful character about God. You only have to look at animals, like lambs gamboling, to realize that the Creator has a delightful sense of humor. If you review how Jesus deals with his disciples, you see that their faults didn't disturb him and that he sometimes made gentle fun of them.

The Divine Indwelling is the basic source of Contemplative Prayer. It needs to be constantly renewed by a practice that focuses our attention on consenting to God's presence and action both within and among us.

> Do you not know that you are the temple of God and that the Spirit of God dwells within you? (1 Corinthians 3:16)

This indwelling presence is the main theological basis for of the practice of Centering Prayer. From another perspective, it is a way of learning God's language, which is silence. Hence in Contemplative Prayer, we adopt a receptive attitude and allow our usual psychological operations to be bracketed during the time that we give to it. Silence is a true and profound form of communication. It draws us by way of attraction to the spiritual level of our being, the level of intuition and our spiritual will, and beyond that level to the true self. The true self is God's idea of who we are.

Centering Prayer reduces the obstacles in us to divine love and enlarges our capacity to engage in the intricacies of the divine dance. When the dance is well executed, it looks like the easiest thing in the world. The exercise of the Fruits of the Spirit builds into daily activities a certain spiritual poise that adapts itself to every situation in an appropriate manner.

One of the Fruits of the Spirit is gentleness. God supervises the amazing activities of the subatomic and supergalactic levels and does so effortlessly. All the works inspired by God partake of that gentleness. For example, one works hard to accomplish God's will, and then steps back and allows the results to happen as if one hadn't done a thing. Efforts to further the Kingdom are not exhausting when they proceed from the inner resource of the Divine Indwelling. Although they may be vigorous in the extreme, inwardly there is no stress. The desire for success or control damages the good works of people who have not accessed this particular Fruit of the Spirit. They think mistakenly, that everything depends on them, including their own progress in the spiritual journey.

It is true we have to reduce the number of obstacles we perceive in ourselves that clearly need putting aside. But God doesn't ask us to *earn* anything. This is one of the errors in a form of religious instruction that teaches or implies that we have to earn God's love or favor. Some people feel they are unworthy of God. Worthiness is not the issue. If we are created out of nothing, what have we got to lose? Nonetheless, because of cultural or religious conditioning, some people feel profoundly unloved. Hence, when it comes to relating to God, they project onto God the way they think of themselves, or the way other people think of them. For example, "This guy is no good. Who could ever love her? Why doesn't someone shoot him?"

My thoughts are not your thoughts. Nor are your ways my ways, says the Lord (Isaiah 55.8).

God doesn't think in these ways at all. The Gospel is not about *earning* the love of God because we already have it. It is a matter of *receiving* it and of being grateful. "The love of God has been poured forth into our hearts by the Holy Spirit that has been given to us" (Romans 5:5).

In Centering Prayer we experience God's presence affirming our basic goodness and, at the same time, leading us towards an ever deeper and honest level of self-knowledge. We are called to give up those things in us that are self-centered and to release our tendency to look to our ego as the great "I" of the universe, which, of course, it is not. Its inverse, the feeling of being unworthy of God, is neurotic and needs to be put in the wastebasket. Everybody needs God. It is not a question of being worthy or not. The issue is: will you, like those people in the third category at the great banquet, come in and sit down with the One who is hosting the party? Will you accept the divine hospitality and join in the dance with God and the other guests? The joint sharing with God of the human condition with its joys and sorrows, its ordinariness, and its deprivations constitutes the dance. These experiences teach us the incomparable benefits of Contemplative Prayer. It is an education in unmerited love.[6] No one is transformed into perfect love on the basis of their deserts, but as a result of the divine largesse.

---

6. *Christian Mysticism: Transcending Techniques,* Marilyn Mallory (Amsterdam: Van Gorcum Assen. 1977).

CHAPTER NINE

The Cost of Christ's Redemptive Activity

Contemplative Prayer is based on the Paschal Mystery, which is the term for the primary work of our redemption: Christ's passion, death, descent into hell, resurrection, and ascension.

As we look at what Christ has taken upon himself in his passion, death and descent into hell, our realization of what the salvation of the world cost him expands exponentially. What do these horrendous events signify? At the very least, they signify that God has taken into himself all our pain, including death, which is the ultimate pain for most people. Moreover, we perceive that God is not just an onlooker of human history and of our individual melodrama, applauding our efforts and lamenting our failures from a safe distance. He *joins* us in our sufferings. In the crucifixion of Jesus, the impossible happens. God dies.

Jesus has taken upon himself all the consequences, private and social, of engaging in acts that trample on the rights of others and our own true good in order to get what we want, or to get away from what we don't want. In perhaps the most extraordinary statement in all of scripture, Paul writes:

> For our sake, God made him to be sin who did not know sin (2 Corinthians 5:21).

God could forgive sin by a simple act of will. It is the *consequences* of sin that are the problem. In general, these are feelings of guilt, humiliation and despair, leading to alienation from God, others, and ourselves. Such dispositions are the natural sanction of going against our conscience. They hurt God, because they hurt us! He loves us and does not will that we suffer needless pain. In proof of this divine disposition, Christ has taken upon himself our psychological and spiritual suffering in his passion, death, and descent into hell and destroyed both sin and its consequences in the abyss of God's infinite mercy.

The anguish of a guilty conscience, if we accept it, is the precise point at which our personal redemption takes place. When we accept the fact of failing God, ourselves, and others—or whatever misconduct lies heavily on our conscience—God takes our suffering into himself and heals it. The very pain we feel, once fully accepted, enables us to become the persons that we really are.

Rather than feeling unworthy of God, we must rather recognize the fact, as the parable of the great banquet reveals, that God *joins* us in our sufferings. Suffering does not reflect God's displeasure, but rather his desire to introduce us to the fullness of his redeeming activity. God's salvific action of course includes not only our personal healing process but extends to the healing of the whole human family. The human family—past, present, and to come—is the object of God's transforming love. It is into this movement of boundless compassion that he draws us as we advance in the spiritual journey. Contemplative prayer, even more than martyrdom, is the most profound participation in the Paschal Mystery. It is, as St. Thérèse of Lisieux puts it, the martyrdom of love.

The Agony in the Garden

Three stages might be distinguished in Christ's assimilation of the human condition in the Paschal Mystery: these are his Agony in the Garden of Gethsemane, his death on the cross, and his descent into hell.

The first stage is the Agony in the Garden. This is the place where Jesus on the night of his arrest withdraws from his disciples about a stone's throw, to watch and pray. The disciples, overcome by sorrow, go to sleep. Jesus is left alone to deal with the realization that he is being asked by the Father, whom he knows as Infinite Goodness, to become the very opposite of who the Father is. For Jesus, this involves identification with the monumental moral corruption of all time, which is the accumulated pile of human suffering of every description. The horrors of every guilty conscience are present in some way in the cup he is asked to drink—not just symbolically, but in fact.

Hell is not so much a place as a state of consciousness in which one feels rejected by God, abandoned by everyone, and hateful to oneself. It also stands for the brutal consequences of inhuman situations including war, terrorism, persecution, exile, imprisonment, grinding poverty, physical and mental illness, desperate loneliness, and every kind of injustice. The mass of human misery, and its source in human malice, is in the cup that the Father is asking him to drink. Jesus cries out, "Father, if it be possible, take this cup from me!" (Matthew 26:39)

To paraphrase this desperate appeal, "Father, if it be possible, take away this abyss of suffering into which I am being plunged. I am *dying of anguish*!" This is the cry of Jesus of human weakness and sinfulness reaching to infinity.

But then Jesus adds, "Nevertheless, not my will but thine be done!" This is the voice of divine love reaching to infinity.

Death on the Cross

The second stage of the Paschal Mystery is the crucifixion. Jesus no longer calls his Father *Abba*, but utters the pitiful plea taken from the first verse of Psalm 22: "My God, my God, why have you forsaken me?" In other words, "How could you reject me, your beloved son?" This question suggests that Jesus on the cross takes upon himself not only all the consequences of sin and human misery, but relinquishes his *identity* as the Son of God. It is this act that manifests—more than any other revelation—a love so great that it is prepared to give up *love itself* for love's sake.

The Descent into Hell

The third stage of the Paschal Mystery is Jesus' descent into hell. According to the theologian Hans Urs von Balthasar (1905–1988), Jesus' descent into hell is the completion of his identification with sin and consequently the precise moment of our redemption.

If Jesus "was made sin," he was not just bearing the physical and mental consequences of alienation, rejection, and desolation that are the natural sanctions of our personal sins or complicity in social sin. He must have experienced the spiritual pain of becoming the opposite of God. The greatest pain of hell is being in the presence of infinite goodness and love, with the realization of having betrayed it. The horror of facing God in that state would constitute a far greater suffering than hell itself; it would be excruciating beyond comprehension. For one with such a disposition, it would be a great mercy *not* to be in God's presence.

When we act against our conscience, we normally have

negative feelings about ourselves and are ashamed to venture into God's presence or to think of God. Our lack of confidence is what causes God suffering. When we accept these negative feelings and turn to God for pardon, we relieve it. For our pain is his pain. He takes away the sins of the world by forgiving everyone and everything. The *consequences* of sin, however—guilt, self-rejection, and self-hatred—are inherent to the human condition. We have the freedom to hang onto these poisonous dispositions. But Christ's identification with them takes them away as soon as we accept responsibility for them and give ourselves to him just as we are.

What we most despise in ourselves may be the most direct route to divine union. God wills that we forgive ourselves for our past mistakes and for whatever unwanted memories are burdening our consciences. A few examples might be: "I didn't do well by my children" . . . "As a soldier, I shot a helpless prisoner" . . . "How could I have abandoned my family?"

The Divine Suffering

Jesus must have known that in becoming sin—the opposite of all that the Father is—he was causing the Father infinite pain—the pain of rejection by His own beloved Son. Thus, the passion and death of Jesus is the passion and death of the Father as well.

Jesus must have been aware that *becoming sin*, even at the express will of the Father, would cause his *Abba* infinite suffering. For that meant he would be rejecting the Father's infinite love for him. To paraphrase the desperate prayer of Jesus in the Garden of Gethsemane, "Father, how can you ask me to become sin? For that will cause you infinite pain."

Of its very nature sin is separation from God. For Jesus, drinking the chalice meant separation from his identity as God's beloved Son. Further, and more poignantly, Jesus' identification with sin meant the rejection of the Father's love itself, thereby causing the Father suffering transcending every physical, mental, and spiritual torment. This is *divine* suffering, a wound directed at the very heart of God and striking at the essence of divinity itself. *It is the rejection of all that the Father is.* But the motive is a love for the Father greater than Love itself.

Since the Father contains all possibilities, was it not inevitable, given the humility of God, that the possibility of being rejected by the One whom the Father (*Abba*) most loved, would actually happen?

Jesus' words, "Not my will but thine be done," express his total acceptance of the Father *just as he is*, who at that supreme moment is prepared to let go of his only begotten Son, the beloved, for the salvation of the world.

"As the Father has loved me, so I have loved you" (John 15:9). The Son is prepared to pass on the same love that he receives from the Father—a love that transcends even rejection and manifests itself as unconditional and everlasting.

Hell as a state of consciousness bears witness to the

alienation and rejection that Jesus, by being made sin, suffered in his descent into hell. Submitting to the process of identification with sin and sinners, Jesus manifests the humility of the Father in the most sublime manner. By taking away the sins of the world and transforming sin itself into unconditional love, Jesus reveals God's will to share the divine life with us to the fullest possible extent, making us, insofar as possible, equal to Himself. Among the Greek Fathers, this is called "divinization."

The Grace of the Resurrection

Jesus dies in the unresolved double bind between identification with the human condition and the loss of his conscious union with the Father. Jesus' resurrection is the Father's response. The Resurrection opens for us, as well as for Jesus, a totally new life. It is the decisive and determining moment in human history. As a result, divine union as an abiding state of consciousness is now accessible to every human being.

As Christ passes into his glorification, he incorporates us into his own glorified body and shares with us his divine happiness. *Alleluia* is the song of resurrection. It is the cry of those in whom the Resurrection is taking place interiorly. Praise, gratitude and boundless confidence in the risen Christ erupt into the ecstatic experience of divine union. "Christ is risen!" is not merely the cry of a few historical witnesses. It is the cry of all the people throughout the centuries who have realized Christ *rising in them*, not in the form of a passing enthusiasm, but in the form of an *unshakable conviction*. The light of Christ radiating from the Paschal Candle reveals in a ritual manner our abiding union with him and its power to transform every aspect of our lives.

The Grace of the Ascension

The grace of the Ascension offers a still more incredible union, a more entrancing invitation to unlimited life and love. This is the invitation to enter into the cosmic Christ—into his divine person, the Word of God, who has always been present in the world in a saving way because of God's foreknowledge of his incarnation, death, and resurrection. Christ is "the true light which enlightens everyone coming into the world" (John 1:9)—the God who is secretly at work in the most unexpected and hidden ways. This is the Christ who disappears in his Ascension beyond the clouds (Acts 1:9), not into some geographical location, but into the heart of all creation. In particular, Christ penetrates the very depths of our being, our separate-self sense melts into his divine Person, and we are empowered to act under the direct influence of his Spirit. Thus, even if we drink a cup of soup or walk down the street, it is Christ living in us, transforming us and the world from within. This transformation appears in the guise of ordinary things and of our seemingly insignificant daily routines. As Paul expressed it, "I live no longer I, but Christ lives in me" (Galatians 2:20).

The Ascension is Christ's return to the center of all creation where he dwells now in his glorified humanity. The mystery of this Presence is hidden throughout creation and in every part of it. At some moment of history, which prophecy calls the Last Day, our eyes will be opened and we will see reality as it is, which we know now only by faith. That faith reveals that Christ, dwelling at the center of all creation and of each individual member of it, is transforming it and bringing it back, in union with himself, into the bosom of the Father. Thus, the maximum glory of the Trinity is achieved through the maximum sharing of the divine life with every creature according to its capacity. This is:

> The plan of the mystery hidden for ages past in God
> who created all things (Ephesians 3:9).

The grace of the Ascension is the uninhibited faith that believes that God's will is being done no matter what happens. It believes that creation is already glorified, though in a hidden manner, as it awaits the full revelation of the children of God. The grace of the Ascension enables us to perceive the irresistible power of the Spirit transforming everything into Christ despite any and all appearances to the contrary. In the misery of the ghetto, in the horror of the battlefield and prison camp; in the family torn by dissension; in the loneliness of the orphanage, old-age home, or hospital ward—whatever seems to be disintegrating into ever grosser forms of evil—the light of the Ascension is burning with irresistible power. This is one of the greatest intuitions of faith. This faith finds Christ not only in the beauty of nature, art, human friendship and the service of others, but also in the malice and injustice of people or institutions, and in the inexplicable suffering of the innocent. Even there it finds the same infinite love expressing the hunger of God for humanity and a corresponding hunger of humanity for God—a hunger that he intends to satisfy.

This is why Paul does not hesitate to cry out with his triumphant faith in the Ascension of Jesus, "Christ is all in all!" (Colossians 3:11), meaning *now*, not just in the future. At this very moment we too have the grace to see Christ's light shining in our hearts, to feel his exquisite Presence within us, and to perceive in every event—even in the most disconcerting—the presence of his light, life, and love. The sacred humanity of Jesus as well as all creation has been affirmed forever by the Resurrection. Through our union with Christ, we share in this grace as co-heirs with him. Through the grace of the Ascension, we become God without ceasing to be the *unique* manifestations of God's goodness that we are. As attachment to our individual false selves diminishes, our true identity grows stronger and manifests who God is as well as who God intends us to be.

CHAPTER TEN

Prayer in Secret

How are we to reach what Paul calls "the deep knowledge of God" (Colossians 1:9; 2:3; 3:4–11), by which he means the experiential knowledge of God, or what the Christian tradition calls "contemplation"? It is the latter that makes us sensitive to the divine mysteries. Though we cannot explain them with our conceptual apparatus, they are just as real as anything that we can see, feel, think, or imagine.

Here is where Jesus' wisdom saying about how to pray comes to our assistance. Wisdom sayings in general are not normally to be taken literally. They are metaphorical and meant to awaken us intuitively to depths of meaning and truth that ordinary discourse cannot articulate. In the Sermon on the Mount Jesus teaches:

> If you want to pray, enter your inner room, close the door, and pray to your *Abba* in secret, and your *Abba* who sees in secret will reward you (Matthew 6:6).

The first term to be investigated in this saying is the name Jesus gives to the Ultimate Reality. He calls It not just "Father," which in the Old Testament means the Source of everything that is. Rather, he calls the Father, *Abba*, an Aramaic word for "daddy." As we have already pointed out, Jesus in his teaching is addressing the prevailing mindset of his time that God was utterly transcendent, remote, the rewarder of good and the punisher of evil, available only at sacred times and places, and mediated by people with sacred credentials such as prophets, priests, and rabbis. These presuppositions are *not* what Jesus meant by the term *Abba*. In fact, he deliberately subverts the identification of the God of Israel with the God of armies and the God of strict justice. This of course is not to say that God is unjust. It means rather that he is not *just* just! The term *Abba* affirms that God is primarily the God of infinite mercy, whose power is in the service of divine love and whose infinite transcendence is equaled by his infinite immanence. This is the God whom one encounters in Contemplative Prayer.

Accordingly, the primary attitude that Jesus suggests we bring to prayer in secret is the realization that God is *Abba*: close, concerned, nurturing, bending over us with boundless protection, tenderness and love. These are the convictions to cultivate in order to enter with confidence into the "inner room." If we have never tasted the experience of God, we might have some hesitations about what this might be like. If we have brought with us from early childhood negative ideas and feelings about God, we may not really want to enter the inner room. Perceiving God as dangerous or even as a kind of monster, like the gods of the Near East in Jesus' time, would introduce a serious obstacle to accepting the invitation to friendship with God. Nobody is going to seek friendship with someone of whom they are scared to death.[7]

A certain choice of scriptural passages needs to be imparted to people who are considering the spiritual journey, especially those who have been psychologically damaged by a catechesis in which negative images about God have been emphasized.

Prayer as Relationship with God

A second important term to understand in this text is the word *pray*. Jesus leads off by saying: "If you want to pray. . . ." In teaching the practice of Centering Prayer, we emphasize prayer as relationship. Whatever one does by way of prayer, ritual, or service toward others, it is essential that one's actions come from a relationship with God characterized by trust and love.

We hear a lot about fear in the scriptures in both the

---

7. In presenting the truths of faith to children, one has to keep in mind how delicate their understanding is and how easily they can associate negative ideas of God with frightening images that they have seen on television or the Internet. The natural tendency of children is to trust God, especially if their parents are windows onto God's goodness manifested by their love for each other and their children. Such an example is an enormous gift for human growth and emotional stability. Without it children may spend the rest of their lives recovering from childhood.

Old and New Testaments. "Fear" is a technical term in scripture and does not normally mean the feeling of fear. It is best translated as reverence, awe, or wonder. An even more accurate rendering might be "the continuous awareness of God's presence." To be always aware of God is to take refuge in God's protection at all times. The last thing the term "fear" implies is to look upon God as dangerous. Like the idea that we are unworthy of God's love, the feeling of fear in relation to God must be firmly put in the wastebasket.

When Jesus says, "If you want to pray," he means "If you want to move beyond signs, wonders, and spiritual consolations in your practice, try this formula." In this way, the essential part of prayer, which is the way one relates to God, will gradually move beyond simple acquaintanceship, and the awkwardness that goes with it, to friendliness in which one can be at ease and converse with God any time, in any place, and in one's own words. It will eventually lead to committing oneself and one's whole life to God and opening oneself to the transformative process of divine union.

Prayer, whatever form it may take, is thus an expression of one's habitual relationship to God. Its translation into prayerful action is dependent on that relationship. The divine invitation might be stated in this way: "If you would like to access the deeper knowledge of God and enter into the process that leads to divine union, then enter your inner room as a first step."

The First Step

Some translations for "inner room" have "private room" to describe what Jesus is talking about. However, only the rich had private rooms in those days. This passage is pointing to a spiritual, not a physical location. This is how the Desert Fathers and Mothers of the Fourth century in Egypt understood this passage.[8] It means to let go of the ordinary psychological awareness of everyday life with its tumult, noise, worries, and the various commentaries that go on in our heads about people, events, and our emotional reactions to them. Letting go of the stimulation to think about anything will enable us to enter the spiritual level of our being of which the inner room is the symbol. This intuitive level is inclined to silence. It is closer to the innermost center of our being which is the true Self, and to the Trinity, the Source of our being at every level—body, soul and spirit.

Jesus recommends letting go of our ordinary ways of relating to reality in favor of a new way of relating that is both liberating and unifying. When we are locked into our ordinary psychological awareness, we are dominated by our experiences—events and people entering and leaving our lives and our emotional reactions to them—and we cannot respond fully to reality or evaluate it objectively. In addition, we are constantly influenced by the values of the culture in which we live, and by what people think of

8. cf. Appendix I, page 129, for the text of John Cassian which interprets Matthew 6:6.

us or don't think of us. The tyranny of over-identification with what is going on at the surface of our awareness prevents us from experiencing the intuitive level that of its very nature tends to be more peaceful, calm, and open to the presence and guidance of the Divine Indwelling.

Notice that Jesus' suggestion implies letting go of the stimulation that comes through our senses, memory, imagination and mental faculties, and to treat them all with complete disregard. In other words, we are not to *engage* with thoughts of any kind during the time of prayer. A "thought" in Centering Prayer terminology has a very generic meaning. It includes *any perception at all*: body sensations, sense perceptions, feelings, images, memories, plans, concepts, reflections, and emotions. All these "thoughts" are deliberately left behind in order to enter the inner room. In Centering Prayer we do not resist thoughts that come down the stream of consciousness. At the same time, we do not hang on to thoughts or react emotionally to them. And when we notice we are engaged with thoughts of any kind, we return ever so gently to the Sacred Word.

This advice emphasizes how firmly we need to let go of external stimuli while we are doing this practice. The inner room, as we saw, is not so much a place as an interior disposition of openness and surrender to God. Centering Prayer can be done anywhere, anytime, and even in situations where there may be a lot of noise. In the beginning, external silence and solitude are very helpful in order to develop the habit of listening to God's presence beyond the noises and preoccupations of everyday life or the particular environment we may be in. With practice we learn to integrate external noises into our prayer without either resisting them or paying any attention to them.

The Second Step

To this first step, Jesus adds the further injunction: "Close the door." Jesus' recommendation obviously requires a choice. It means that, at least in our will, we let go of ordinary, everyday awareness for the whole time of the prayer period. If thoughts keep coming down the stream of consciousness, as they inevitably do, we do not get disturbed, but simply disregard them. With time, the promptness with which we let them go dismantles the mental habits of a lifetime. In the beginning, any perception that comes down the stream of consciousness is likely to set off a response from one or other of our instinctual needs: survival and security, affection and esteem, and power and control. Without a regular daily practice of silent prayer, we are unaware of how much energy we put into those projects. The need for the gratification of one of the emotional programs in some people actually turns into a *demand*. We then expect others to respect our outrageous expectations or plans for the gratification of our emotional programs. It is not the desires for the gratification of our instinctual needs that are wrong; they are necessary for our survival in early childhood. Our mistake is to invest them with exaggerated expectations and to seek happiness through the gratification of these childish programs in adult life where they cannot possibly work. As the enormous energy we put into satisfying these instinctual needs diminishes, we have vastly more energy for the spiritual journey and for the service of others.

God's first language is silence. As soon as we put the deep knowledge of God into words, we have interpreted it. Every translation is in some degree an interpretation. The Mystery that we are accessing is available for us just as it is, not as we think it is, or as we want it to be.

The Interior Dialogue

To close the door to the inner room is an invitation to discontinue our interior dialogue. That means not to think *about* the things we are perceiving through the senses or reflecting upon with our rational apparatus. In practice, we stop harboring expectations or goals for our prayer period—such as to repeat the sacred word continuously, to have no thoughts at all, to make our minds a blank, to enjoy spiritual experiences, and to feel peaceful or consoled. All such desires for particular results are "thoughts" in the umbrella sense in which we use this term in the Centering Prayer practice. As particular perceptions, they are not appropriate during the time we are in the inner room. In practice, whenever in Centering Prayer we have a particular thought that engages our attention, we reaffirm our original *intention* of closing the door by returning ever so gently to the sacred word.

Of what does the interior dialogue normally consist? It is that discussion we have with ourselves that goes on continuously twenty-four hours a day, in which we evaluate and comment on what is happening with regard to events, people entering and leaving our lives and our emotional reactions to them. This endless stream of commentaries, judgments, and desires can be more disruptive of interior silence than the ordinary level of awareness that we chose to leave behind when we began our prayer.

Given that we have long-established and deep-rooted habits of thinking and reacting from early childhood, we have to be patient with ourselves in trying to moderate our reflective apparatus with its tendency to think about anything that comes to mind. The humble acceptance of our weakness is one of the principal disciplines of Centering Prayer. It is at the same time a relationship of boundless confidence in God. We believe that God is already present. Hence, there is no place to go to find him and no need to run away from ourselves.

The Third Step

Finally, Jesus says: "Pray to your *Abba* in secret." Notice in this formula the cascading movement toward ever deeper levels of interior silence. First, we let go of external stimuli. Then we relinquish the interior dialogue with ourselves. Finally, we enter the stillness of prayer in secret.

This might be called the silence of self. "Perfect prayer," according to St. Anthony the Great, "is not to know that you are praying." It is to forget self and to let go for the whole time of the prayer period all self-reflection including, so far as possible, self-consciousness itself.

Notice the reason for prayer in secret that Jesus implies. If we are to access the God who sees in secret and is in secret, we have to enter into the same kind of secrecy. God is so close that we do not have any faculty to interpret the divine presence. Only pure faith beyond thoughts, feelings, and reflections can access it.

The inner room gives us a chance to take a vacation from ourselves. There is nothing so relaxing. It is a much better place to go than Florida, Hawaii, or anywhere else, because it is our *thoughts*, in the broad sense described above, and especially those with an emotional charge to them, that give us the most trouble. They are often a form of torture. Our choice at the beginning of prayer to consent to God's presence and action repeated throughout the period of prayer by returning to the sacred symbol, will itself become a habit. It will gradually undermine the urgency of the emotional programs for happiness. Our energy, instead of being wasted on trivia, will become available to respond to the needs of others and the liberation of all that is creative in our own natural endowment.

CHAPTER ELEVEN

The Reward of Prayer in Secret

The reward of prayer in secret in the wisdom saying of Jesus (Matthew 6:6) is the deep knowledge of God leading to living continuously in the divine presence. This presence has always been with us, but it has been elusive, not because God is elusive, but because of the energy we have invested in self-centered preoccupations and projects. Thus it is we who are seldom present to God. Preoccupation with thinking *about* particular objects, body sensations, concepts, memories, plans, and feelings hinders the development of interior silence.

The Way of Pure Faith

The way of pure faith is a giant leap of spiritual development beyond the level of those who seek enlightenment or spiritual consolation and the devout who want "signs and wonders." Pure faith is a movement beyond the limitations of our attachments. It is liberation from the desire that God fit into these naïve criteria. God is too transcendent to be perceived as he truly is by any of our faculties, but that does not mean that he is not present. It simply means that we are already in God's presence. We can't in fact get away from it. There is no place to go to get away from God because wherever we go, God will be there ahead of us.

> Where can I hide from your spirit?
> From your presence, where can I flee?
> If I ascend to the heavens, you are there.
> If I lie down in Sheol, you are there too.
> If I fly with the wings of dawn
> And alight beyond the sea
> Even there your hand will guide me.
> Your right hand holds me fast (Psalm 139:7–10).

Prayer in secret implies no *deliberate* self-reflection. We are normally aware of ourselves all the time and in every situation. Consciousness of self is the last bastion of the ego. Under its influence, we never quite experience the present moment. The ego acts as a kind of bridge from the past to the future, hindering us from ever being where God actually is, which is in the present moment.

Part of the discipline of Centering Prayer is that, at least during the time of our prayer, we stay in the present moment. Anything from the past or the future that passes through our awareness is simply disregarded. "Letting go" is another name for this effortless practice. But we don't just let go for the sake of letting go. We let go as a gift to God. In other words, our relationship with God prompts us to let go of all thoughts as they arise and to give them to God as gifts.

The divine action is healing; it is never a punishment. If Centering Prayer is painful, boring or tedious at times and we seem to be going nowhere, these may be signs that we have temporarily stopped letting go. All we have to do when thoughts are urgent or persistent is return, ever so gently, to the sacred symbol we have chosen as the expression of our intention to spend this time with God and to accept the divine action within us. This acceptance includes the flow of thoughts we cannot change, however repulsive these may be.

What Goes on in the Inner Room?

Two things take place in the inner room. The first is the affirmation of our basic goodness; the second is the purification of the unconscious. The latter is the healing of the repressed emotional material of a lifetime that has been stored in the body as in a warehouse. I call this process of healing the "unloading" of the unconscious. Until it is evacuated, the energy of negative material continues to influence our behavior and decisions all through life. This pattern is challenged and gradually dismantled if we accept Christ's invitation to join him in the radical healing and transformation of our spiritual faculties (intellect and will) into the divine mode of functioning. The process of transformation takes place primarily through the exercise of the Theological Virtues of faith, hope, and charity, enhanced by the Fruits and Seven Gifts of the Spirit.

The secrecy I was speaking about is related to this attitude of accepting the divine action. The divine action is both affirming and confrontational. The emotional wounds of a lifetime normally have to come to consciousness if they are to be healed. They may arise during Centering Prayer as primitive emotions that have no relation to the immediate past. This fact is the surest sign that they are emerging from the unconscious. Through the deep rest of Centering Prayer, the body receives permission, so to speak, to evacuate the undigested emotional material of a lifetime. Since it is unconscious, it has never been dealt with. It is sitting there in our psyche like an undigested meal on our stomach.

The deeper the interior silence, the greater the physical rest the body experiences. The rest is partially due to not thinking deliberately. It is also due to the increase of trust in God that is the result of the affirmation of our basic goodness communicated to our spirit in the inner room. This affirmation may take the form of a sense of God's presence, interior peace, or being forgiven, that everything is okay, that God is taking care of us and that there is nothing to worry about. All of these are different means that God uses to reassure us not only when we are in the inner room, but also in the course of everyday life. God's desire is to heal the depths of our unconscious motivation that is the chief obstacle to divine love. In this way, our whole being can be filled with the Holy Spirit and the in-pouring of divine love. Paul puts it in this way: "The love of God is poured forth in our hearts by the Holy Spirit who is given to us" (Romans 5:5).

Every time we let go of some glob of undigested emotional material repressed in early childhood, the Holy Spirit rushes in and fills that space by increasing or activating the Fruits and Gifts of the Spirit. Sometimes, after the period of prayer and because of the new space that is now present within us, our mind clarifies. We begin to see certain dynamics of our unconscious that had been hidden from us, or how much energy we put into trying to make the emotional programs for happiness work. No amount of effort to make them work ever succeeds. However, the more at peace we are and the more deeply we rest in God during prayer, the faster and more completely the undigested emotional material of a lifetime is evacuated. This is called in the Christian Contemplative tradition, the purification of the soul. Modern psychology since Sigmund Freud (1856–1939) has recognized the existence of the unconscious. This is an enormous insight not only for medicine and psychotherapy, but for the Spiritual Journey. We can now recognize that growth in mental health is also growth in the spiritual life.

When we are immersed during Centering Prayer in primitive feelings or a bombardment of afflictive thoughts, all we have to do is to accept them and give them to God. In every Roman Catholic mass, the following words are recited: "Lamb of God, you take away the sins of the world, have mercy on us." If Christ has taken away our sins, where are they? They don't exist; we only think they do. In actual fact, as soon as we sincerely ask pardon for our sins, they are instantly annihilated in the abyss of God's infinite mercy.

Freedom for the Exercise of the Fruits of the Spirit

Freedom from the effects of negative energies in the unconscious makes room, as we saw, for the Fruits of the Spirit—especially charity (the kind of selfless love that was discussed in chapter 5), peace (the peace that Paul says "surpasses all understanding"), and joy (the abiding sense of well-being). Our residual fascination with values that are rooted in the false self have to go if we wish to "enter through the narrow gate" (Matthew 7:13) or "go through the eye of the needle" (Matthew 19:24) into the Kingdom. The latter requires letting go of useless baggage including our possessive attitudes, emotional programs for happiness, and over-identification with the particular group to which we belong.

We witness this healing process taking place on many occasions recorded in the Gospels. Jesus used exactly the same therapy with his disciples and the people of his time that he now uses with us. Just as effectively, patiently and lovingly, he brings to our attention the attitudes and behavior that we need to correct or, more exactly, to allow him to correct, in order to move to deeper levels of the knowledge and love of God.

As we reflect on Jesus' exhortation to enter the inner room, we see that it is, first of all, a process of liberation from the false self. In the short term, it is an oasis in daily life in which we can be refreshed by the values of the inner room and move towards establishing habits of letting go of attitudes and behaviors that are inappropriate or harmful both in prayer and action. The reason why thoughts are so attractive is that, when we are engaged in thinking, we don't normally think of what is causing the pain. We can cover over painful aspects of interior states by constantly thinking about something else. If things from the past or that are done to us in the present strike us as unfair, we no longer identify with these judgments, give way to angry feelings, and act them out. We are learning that we are *not* our feelings. We *have* feelings, but we no longer over-identify with them.

For example, when we say, "I'm angry!" this is not correct! *We* are not angry; we have angry *feelings*. Once we do not identify with angry feelings, we can change them. With God's help, we can let them go by. We can refrain from projecting them onto others and blaming them for making us mad.

With the growing level of faith and the evacuation of the obstacles to divine love, the Fruits of the Spirit manifest themselves more regularly in daily life. For example, goodness as a Fruit of the Spirit is the capacity to see God in everything, whether in people, nature, or events. When we perceive God in a storm, the storm takes on a wholly different quality. Christ is in every kind of storm including those that set off feelings of indignation, resentment, and rage.

These emotions, of course, need to be moderated. The Divine Therapy not only tends to regulate our experience of prayer but also expands the walls of our inner room to include the whole of life. Everyday life becomes an opportunity to recognize the dynamics of our unconscious motivation. As we become more skilled in letting go of thoughts, we perceive that they are often defense mechanisms that conceal some emotional pain that needs to come to consciousness in order to be healed. Since feelings are only energy, as soon as we allow ourselves to feel and accept them, they tend to dissipate and are often gone forever.

Once in a while, some problem coming from deep in our childhood arises that may need psychotherapy. Jesus, speaking of his role as healer, said: "Those who are healthy do not need a physician, but the sick do" (Luke 5:31). If psychiatry had been known in his day, he would certainly have accepted it as part of his healing ministry.

CHAPTER TWELVE

What Is Divine Therapy?

The false self is based on two foundational pillars: one is the energy invested in the emotional programs for happiness and the other is the tendency to over-identify with the particular group from which we come or to which we belong. All through the ages, there has been a certain stratification of society in which one had to accept values that were pre-programmed by family, custom or the larger community. Anyone who did not submit would be ostracized. The cultural straightjacket of over-identification with our particular group is something that Jesus invites us to break out of with this strong warning:

> If anyone comes to me without hating his father and mother, wife and children, brothers and sisters, and even his own life, he cannot be my disciple (Luke 14:26).

This saying is an important aspect of Jesus' teaching

about repentance. To repent is to change the direction in which we are looking for happiness. In this saying, Jesus exhorts us to relinquish our over-identification with our group so that we can be free to follow the values of the Gospel and our own conscience, and not be fearful of unsettling the group to which we belong by questioning or opposing its values.

Having reached a certain detachment from our family, roles, profession, business and social group, we have to let go of our over-identification with who we think we are. This is a problem for people with special roles like parents, ministers, politicians and in ancient times, kings and nobles who completely identified with their positions of prestige, power, or wealth. As we have seen, Jesus in the parables tends to undermine the social structures of his time and to subvert the unjust values on which they were based. The thrust of Jesus' parables is to take down barriers of all kinds and to enable people to experience their unity as members of the whole human family and not just with their own family, ethnic group, nation, peer group, or religion. As Paul sees it:

> There is neither Jew nor Greek, there is neither
> slave nor free person, there is not male and female;
> for you are all one in Christ Jesus (Galatians 3:28).

At a certain point in our lives, we come to what is called "the mid-life crisis." This is the time when our overambitious aspirations for success, fame, and fortune are drained of their attraction. Whatever symbols in the culture appealed to us as the ideal gratification of our emotional programs for happiness are more or less shattered. Actually, following the tragic events of September 11, 2001 and the attack on the World Trade Center and the Pentagon, many people asked themselves: "Why do I bother to go to work? Why am I struggling so hard to climb the social and economic ladders? Why am I going to all this trouble when every place I go is unsafe and the future is so uncertain?" The old security systems we were familiar with and the fact that no foreign army has reached our shore since the War of 1812 have given Americans a disproportionate sense of security in a number of ways, especially in our invulnerability to external attack.

As the onset of the mid-life crisis comes, people's families are usually in a state of flux. The children have moved out and the couple is back to living with just each other. It is a time when many people get divorced, when second careers are initiated, or the purpose of life is profoundly questioned. In other words, people have not found in their emotional programs for happiness, expressed in the symbols of the culture, what they had hoped for and expected.

During this time, some who can afford it seek psychotherapy, or take whatever the contemporary pill is that helps them feel somewhat calm. The truth is that they will never be permanently at peace with themselves until they face head-on what their real problems are. The purpose of chemicals, at least as was believed in psychotherapy until recently, is to put troubled patients in a normal state of mind by chemical means, so that they can then begin to deal with the emotional issues that are behind their mental distress through some form of psychotherapy. For some people, however, there may be a chemical imbalance for which a prescribed drug is needed, in much the same way that a thyroid deficiency needs lifelong treatment with a replacement therapy for the normal functioning of a person.

If the mid-life crisis doesn't work to solve the problems that stem from over-identification with our group associations, nature has other means of disengaging us from excessive loyalties and the roles that we played in order to gratify our emotional programs for happiness. One of these is old age, when we may become feeble and perhaps a little senile. The number of people relying on us declines, and eventually children wind up taking care of their parents, sometimes to the point of taking care of them as if they were actually children. Then comes the crisis of moving to an old age or nursing home. In any case, if we do not freely give up our former roles, they are forcibly taken from us in the relentless aging process. The question arises: Why not detach ourselves from our group loyalties sooner so that we can enjoy the freedom of choosing the measure in which we are going to belong to a particular group, and the freedom to withdraw if its values are not in accord with those of our conscience? This is the call of the Gospel to follow Christ and to begin the spiritual journey.

If the factors of personal diminishment recommended by Jesus are postponed, there is the possibility that the dying process itself may prove to be transforming. When the brain dies, that is the end of the false self and all its support systems. We don't know much about the dying process—for example, when death actually occurs or how long our spirit lingers close to the body. These still remain mysteries. According to contemporary research, there seem to be a variety of possibilities. Whatever death is, it may be the moment in which for the first time we can make a fully free choice. When the brain dies, we are no longer influenced, at least to the same degree as in this life, by the emotional programs for happiness, by dependency upon a group, or by the roles with which we over-identified throughout our lives.

From this perspective sickness, tragedy, natural and even manmade disasters are not unmitigated evils. For many people they are the only way that the false values they absorbed as children are ever questioned, reevaluated, and put in the wastebasket. This is not to say that there are no values at all in one's roles. It is the *over-identification* with them that makes it difficult or even impossible to fulfill them. Perhaps the only way to become a great parent is to be willing *not* to be one; for example, to let grownup children become whoever they want to be without regard to oneself. A similar letting go process is needed for every role model.

The point of Jesus' wisdom saying about detachment from family, property, and oneself is to expose the false self and its support systems because it is an illusion and cannot work. It fouls up our relationships with God, other people, and ourselves.

Along with the invitation to repent—to change the direction in which we are looking for happiness—comes Jesus' invitation to submit to the Divine Therapy: If you want to be free, he suggests, if you want to heal your relationship with God, with others and yourself, enter your inner room—the office, where the Divine Therapy takes place. Close the door so you don't run away. Quiet your interior dialogue so that you can listen to what the Spirit is saying to you."

The purpose of the Divine Therapy is to enable us to become who we really are. We may be scared of being who we are. Jesus addresses this situation in these words: "If you try to save your life (that is your false self), you will bring yourself to ruin." The false self has no future.

The second half of the saying is, "One who brings himself to nought for me discovers who he is" (Matthew 10:39).[9] The true self is limitless in its spiritual capacity. To bring oneself to no-thing, that is, to no particular

---

9. This translation appears in the readings for the Thirteenth Sunday in Ordinary Time, Cycle A, *The Vatican II Sunday Missal*, copyright 1970 by the Confraternity of Christian Doctrine, Washington, DC.

thing, is to let go of over-identification with one's body, feelings, thoughts, and one's inmost self, as well as friends, relatives, property, and roles. It also means moderating our exaggerated desires for the gratification of our emotional programs for happiness. The Divine Therapy is designed to enable us to negotiate this healing process according to genetic and temperamental factors, our personality and the circumstances of our lives. An enormous Intelligence is guiding us through this process with a love that is unconditional and determined to bring about this healing, whatever the cost to Itself.

The Healing Process

What goes on in the inner room, the office of the Divine Therapist, when we expose our inmost being twice each day to the divine Spirit?

We already distinguished the two primary purposes for this profound healing and transformative process. The first is the affirmation of our basic goodness. When we decide to submit to the Divine Therapy, the first thing that God does is to reassure us that we are respected and loved by God. The idea that we are no good, unlovable or unworthy—beliefs that, as we have seen, may be firmly entrenched from early childhood—is an insult to God. God does not make junk; *we* make junk.

God supports and honors his image within us because it reflects his own goodness. Hell itself cannot destroy this basic goodness. No amount of failure on our part, no amount of subjugation to the human condition, no amount of disregard for our own conscience and the needs and rights of other people, can ever take away our indestructible capacity to recover from the wounds of the human condition and the consequences of our deliberate sins.

The affirmation of our basic goodness is manifested during the time of prayer by a sense of God's presence, of being forgiven, or of being loved by God. This reassurance gives us the courage and strength to drop attractive or repulsive thoughts. During the time of prayer, we do not think *about* thoughts, whether they are perceived as good, bad, or indifferent. Instead, we simply allow them to pass through our awareness and out the other side. Time in this discipline is our friend. If we wait long enough, everything passes. As we let go of thoughts, feelings, and perceptions, we begin to experience a certain level of peace. Immersion in the psychological awareness of everyday life and in our interior dialogue is disturbing and a frequent source of anxiety. As our mind calms down, the number of thoughts, at least under normal conditions, diminishes and we sense the presence of God within as an habitual disposition. Fidelity to the twice-daily periods of Centering Prayer then seems easy or even essential for our well being. At this point in the practice, some people say that they cannot *not* do it. If they miss doing it for a day or two, they feel uneasy, as if an important part of their daily lives were missing.

The Divine Therapy manifests itself in the feeling that everything is basically okay, even though we still feel under the influence of the emotional programs for happiness and our various over-identifications. We know there are things that we should change in our lives, but are not quite ready to do so, or simply don't know how. There are also issues we see need changing that we were not aware of until we began this process. Entering the inner room is an expression of good will that is the principal disposition that God asks of us. "Come and be healed!" is the divine invitation. We open to a new world that is manifested in daily life not only by greater peace, calm, and sometimes joy, but also by a greater concern for others in *practical* ways.

In the Divine Therapy our relationships begin to be healed through the process of dismantling our emotional programs for happiness and dis-identifying with our over-dependency on a particular group. This growing interior freedom also includes moderating our over-identification with our bodies, thoughts, and feelings.

Practicing Centering Prayer on a regular basis enables us to establish a discipline leading to Contemplative Prayer. More and more, the Spirit of God takes over our prayer through the exercise of the contemplative Gifts of the Spirit—Knowledge, Understanding, and Wisdom. The Spirit begins to modify our view of reality, cultural conditioning, and the belief systems that we absorbed in early childhood. I refer here not so much to religious beliefs, but to the beliefs current in the culture or environment that we interiorized during the socialization period from four to eight years of age.

Human beings always act out of some belief system—whether it happens to be true or false, conscious or unconscious. For example, if we believe that we have to please everybody, always attain straight A's in school, and be a high achiever in every undertaking, our emotions will certainly react to the inevitable failure of such expectations. Status symbols and group values are rooted in belief systems. They hinder our freedom to choose what we believe is right, or to do what we really want to do.

CHAPTER THIRTEEN

The Process of Purification

The second purpose of the Divine Therapy is the process of purification. In the ongoing course of the treatment, we are gradually made aware of the dark side of our personality and of the repressed emotional trauma of a lifetime. To state the issue in another way, we are made aware over time of whatever in us is opposed to the image and likeness of God in which we were created. The affirmation of our basic goodness, as sublime as it truly is, is only half the story. At the same time as these affirmations are going on, the Divine Therapist, proportionate to our desire to be healed of our false selves, is taking away the support systems that keep the false self firmly in place. Through external circumstances, but mostly through reducing our attachment to our emotional programs for happiness and our over-identification with our group, God regularly interrupts these delightful spiritual consolations with lengthy periods in which we confront the emotional wounds of a lifetime. Thus, in daily life we are likely to perceive how we project our frustrating emotions on other people so that we don't have to feel them ourselves. Or again we may indulge in various kinds of compensatory activity in which we try to manipulate other people or events to hide from ourselves painful emotional traumas that we may have been subjected to in early life and from which we are continuously running away through one means or another.

The Purification of the Unconscious

The Divine Therapy, through the intensification of our experience of God and the deep rest that occurs from spiritual consolation, loosens up the residue of the painful emotional traumas. In early childhood, in order to escape emotional pain, we are likely to repress these traumas into the unconscious. God gently, but with incomparable skill, brings these emotional wounds and painful truths about ourselves to our attention both during prayer and in the course of daily life.

The Divine Therapeutic process normally takes years to negotiate. It is something like an archeological dig. God works back through our personal history starting where we are now, revealing emotional wounds from each period of our lives all the way back to earliest childhood and even into the womb. In this process God works in such a way as to enable us to accept and surrender our emotional wounds in an ever more thoroughgoing manner. The same painful memories recycle at ever deepening levels, as the process of purification relentlessly pursues its goal of interior freedom.

We may then enjoy a period of peace and a return of the consoling experiences described above. When God thinks we have rested long enough on one of these plateaus, he takes up the work of purification once again, as if to say, "Now let's look at some other significant issues." It may feel as if they were the same issues we thought we had handled long ago. And in a sense they are. But now we are asked to deal with them at a much more profound and comprehensive level. The same old problems like endless scenarios reappear, but now with greater clarity, intensity, final resolution, and interior freedom.

These problems are not really the same problems we may have already faced. We are simply dealing with a deeper level of our unconscious. God mercifully does not ask us to look at the whole sad story of our unconscious attachments all at once or right away. God knows us through and through and does not impose upon us more self-knowledge than we can handle at any one point in our spiritual journey. However, as we become more humble and let go of our need for compensatory activities, the inner light that results in deeper self-knowledge increases. This is the exercise of the Gift of Knowledge, one of the Seven Gifts of the Holy Spirit bestowed on us in Baptism. In Christian contemplative terminology, it initiates the state that John of the Cross calls the Night of Sense.

The Nights of Sense
The Gift of Knowledge is an intuitive awareness (not

reached through reflection and the rational faculties) that spontaneously arises as a result of the growing interior silence we are cultivating in Centering Prayer. It can also be accessed through the prolonged practice of *Lectio Divina*, liturgy, and other forms of prayer. However, a method of preparing for Contemplative Prayer by means of cultivating regular periods of interior silence is more direct and may thus speed up the process. Little by little or perhaps all at once, there is a breakthrough in which we realize, not only that we were made for unlimited happiness, but that happiness can only be found in the God who *is* happiness. This insight relativizes all of the expectations we previously relied upon to find happiness in the gratification of the emotional programs for happiness through the symbols provided by the particular society in which we live. Now we know we cannot find happiness in cultural symbols of security and survival, power and control, or affection and esteem. An enormous freedom opens up inside us; but because we loved our emotional programs so much, we may slip into a period of mourning. The radical dismantling or undermining of the false self and the emotional programs on which it was constructed has begun in earnest.

Since we can no longer hope to find happiness through the former sources of emotional gratification, we move into a period of grief, dryness, and perhaps discouragement. This grieving is the natural reaction to anything we greatly love and then have lost. We hoped, sometimes desperately, that our emotional programs for happiness would work, and now that we know this is not going to happen, we experience depressed feelings. This decisive movement toward holistic health must be carefully distinguished from clinical depression, which is an illness.

We can now identify the Night of Sense as a natural mourning process that occurs in response to the loss of something we greatly loved. Even if we go through it patiently, we feel the stress, the tears coming down our face, the acute disappointment of expectations, and perhaps pervasive discouragement. Most poignantly, we feel that the relationship we had with God has been undermined by something that we don't even know or can't figure out. We need to be aware that these thoughts are just rationalizations or commentaries, interpreting this perplexing and painful experience in a way that our rational faculties can understand. Since nothing like it has ever happened to us before, we may interpret God's apparent absence as the deterioration of our former reassuring and consoling relationship.

If that is the case, we are projecting our grief and confusion onto God. As a result, we are mistakenly convincing ourselves that God is displeased with us. We may even feel rejected by God. Nothing could be further from the truth! God is purifying and healing the mixed motivation in our relationship with the divine. Some aspects of that relationship were under the influence of our emotional programs for happiness that translated easily to the spiritual plane when we first undertook the spiritual journey. The time has now come to serve God without seeking reward in the form of spiritual consolation and special proofs of God's approval. We are called to believe in God's love for us on the basis of pure faith.

The problem that the divine action is addressing is that we were relating to God with mixed motives. We were serving God, yes, and we were inspired by grace. However, there were also human expectations rooted in the unredeemed recesses of our unconscious that the Divine Therapy had not reached yet. All that God asks of us in this situation is to accept the mourning period and to be faithful to prayer no matter what happens. The basic work of the Night of Sense is to undermine the false self at its roots. The ultimate goal, of course, is its death.

The Night of Sense can last a long time, but is not limited to an extended period of mourning. It is the occasion of adjusting to the fact that God is no longer going to give us spiritual consolations on a day-to-day, week-to-week, basis. Rather he is urging us to grow up in virtue of these graces and to take responsibility for manifesting God in whatever ways are appropriate in our daily lives. Under the influence of the Night of Sense, the inner room (that is, the office of the Divine Therapist) begins to expand. The walls go down, and when we leave the inner room, the process of purification follows us around. In other words, it accompanies us as a spiritual presence in daily life. The Divine Therapy goes on in all circumstances, revealing our faults as well as activating the manifold Fruits and the Sevenfold Gifts of the Spirit. Through their exercise, we are more and more aware of the spiritual level of our being and of the God who dwells there, but in such a way that this higher level of consciousness does not interfere with our duties and ordinary activities.

In this situation, it may be helpful to remind ourselves that Jesus instituted the same kind of program of apprenticeship for his disciples. God is not angry with us at all. He expects us to make mistakes. He gives us millions (indeed billions and trillions) of chances. If anything, God likes our weakness because it enables him to exercise his infinite mercy. When Paul prayed earnestly to be delivered from a particularly annoying weakness, God said to him:

> My grace is enough for you, for power is made perfect in weakness (2 Corinthians 12:9).

According to this text, we do God a great favor by accepting our weakness. So there is no reason to be saddened by the fact that we do not measure up to our idealized image of ourselves and of how we should perform in the spiritual journey. That obviously is an ego trip.

The Night of Spirit
The Night of Spirit is a more radical psycho-spiritual treatment. According to St. John of the Cross, it is caused by the infusion of Divine Love. St. John the Baptist refers

to it as the Baptism of the Holy Spirit (John 1:33). This love is now coming no longer through the consoling experiences described above, but through the expansion of pure faith that grows brighter through the darkness of God's seeming absence.

The secret satisfaction that we had taken from the felt consolations of our spiritual exercises is gone. Hereafter, there is a sense of being deprived of all human and divine support. Gone are the human props that we had previously depended upon to sustain our spiritual journey. Our human faculties try to figure this out, saying, "I must have committed a secret sin, displeased God, or God has lost interest in me"—all of which is nonsense. But that is the way the commentaries of the false self function. To these misgivings we must vigorously oppose boundless confidence in God as our *Abba*. Consultation with someone who has gone through this process is a great help at this time.

From several points of view, there is no greater grace than the Night of Spirit. For one thing, we know at last that it is not in ecstatic experiences or highly enlightened states that the essence of Contemplative Prayer resides, but rather in the purification of our own psychological and collective unconscious. This deep purification releases the graces stored in what might be called the *ontological* unconscious, where the spiritual gifts so abundantly bestowed at Baptism are waiting to be activated. As it also purifies the roots of our psychological unconscious, we become convinced that, under certain extreme circumstances, we would be capable of every evil. The entire liberating process enables the Holy Spirit to take over the whole of our lives. If we were constantly having spiritual consolations and ecstatic experiences such as St. Teresa describes in *Interior Castle*, we could not function as ordinary persons. We could not lead an ordinary life. Spiritual consolations are only a phase to orientate us toward levels of divine union that vastly transcend particular or passing experiences. The goal of the Night of Spirit is to bring us to the permanent and continuous awareness of God's presence and of our abiding union with him. Our emotional programs for happiness based on the instinctual needs of the child have finally found their true home: God is our security, God is our Beloved, God is our freedom.

The Night of Spirit completes the work of the Night of Sense. The Night of Spirit is a more profound sharing in the passion of Christ. It assimilates us to the Paschal Mystery: that is, to Christ's passion, death, descent into hell, resurrection and ascension. The Ascension is the celebration of Christ's glory at the right hand of the Father. Our assimilation to the mystery of the Ascension is the completion of Christian transformation. From this perspective, the Transforming Union is the beginning of a new life. Perhaps we could say it is the true Christian life, that is, the abiding state in which Christians are meant to participate and to manifest in this life.

CHAPTER FOURTEEN

The Stages of Contemplative Prayer

The Centering Prayer practice consists of introducing silently a sacred word of one or two syllables as a gesture of consenting to God's presence and action within. An inward glace toward God performs a similar function. The sacred glance is not an image or a particular concept, but simply turning inwardly with our will toward the secret Presence that we believe is within us. Our intention and consent to God can also be expressed by noticing our breathing as a symbol of the Spirit. In both Hebrew (*ruach*) and Greek (*pneuma*), "spirit" means "breath." Noticing our breath in Centering Prayer is not an act of concentration on the breathing process or following our breathing physiologically. Since we have to breathe anyway, it is easy just to be briefly aware of it. All three gestures are hallowed by the Christian contemplative tradition as expressions of our intention to consent to God's presence and action within; or more exactly, to consent to *God's* intentionality, which is to transform us into Godself.

As we practice Centering Prayer on a daily basis, the capacity to let go of attractive or negative thoughts increases. The act of letting go becomes more prompt. As this promptness becomes habitual, there are moments in which we are aware that we are not interested in any thought at all, even the most interesting or attractive. In those moments, our mind and hearts are able to respond more fully to the movements of the Spirit.

The fact that one is not attracted to thoughts passing along the stream of consciousness during Centering Prayer is not a judgment. It is not an act of reasoning and still less is it a conscious choice. It happens spontaneously and intuitively. One is aware that thoughts of various kinds are going by such as body sensations, sense perceptions, feelings, memories, plans, concepts, images, reflections—all that we call "thoughts" in the Centering Prayer practice. Nevertheless, we feel an inner reassurance that these thoughts are not interfering with our interaction with God. Centering Prayer is a movement inspired by grace from conversation to communion, from activity to receptivity. This receptivity is not just passivity, but has a welcoming quality to it, like the special way one receives an honored guest or loved one into one's home. This receptive disposition with its welcoming quality enables the contemplative Gifts of the Spirit to take root and gradually take over our prayer. The Spirit then dispenses with all methods and guides us during the time of prayer from start to finish.

The Prayer of Interior Recollection

The occasional experience of freedom from attachment to thoughts is the beginning of Contemplative Prayer in the classic sense of the term. This grace at first is still tenuous, so there is an alternation between the experience of interior silence and our own very gentle activity of returning to the sacred symbol when we are engaged with thoughts. Being aware of thoughts while being free from engaging with them is a taste of true freedom. As a result, love, peace and joy—the first three Fruits of the Spirit mentioned by Paul—manifest in our activities and relationships outside formal times of prayer.

The experience during Centering Prayer when one notices that one is not interested in one's thoughts is a sign that Contemplative Prayer is taking root. Interior silence becomes more and more profound, pervasive, and peaceful. The gift of interior silence is sown in us as a precious seed through the daily practice of Centering Prayer and comes to full bloom in "prayer in secret."

Suppose that the Spirit has grasped our will in such a way that we are not interested in the usual psychological panorama that goes on in our imagination during a particular period of Centering Prayer. The reason we are not interested in any kind of thought (in the general sense of the term) is that the Spirit is emitting from the center of our inmost being a spiritual attraction that might be compared to the odor of perfume. This, of course, is just a metaphor, but it is a favored one among certain Fathers of the Church, who saw in the natural attraction to the scent of sweet-smelling flowers a figure of how the Divine Presence, by its very nature, attracts our spiritual will. Our spirit wants to follow this delightful sense of presence to its source. Perhaps this is what the Psalmist was experiencing when he wrote, "Taste and see that the Lord is good" (Psalm 34:8).

The Prayer of Quiet

As the attraction to silence, solitude and inner peace insinuates itself more frequently into our consciousness during Centering Prayer, the Spirit may grasp our spiritual will more strongly than by a simple attraction, resulting in what St. Teresa of Avila calls "the Prayer of Quiet."[10] This does not mean we have no thoughts at all. On the contrary, sometimes feelings and images are more intense and disagreeable than ever. At this level of Contemplative Prayer, the Spirit does not grasp our imagination and discursive faculties, but only the will. The will is aware of being united to God in some deep and satisfying way, while an annoying barrage of thoughts may be going on at the same time in our memory or imagination. There may be a fear that by pursuing some particular thought, we will lose the delicious sense of God's presence. That presence manifests itself by a certain delight that is subdued but strong enough that one would like to prolong

---

10. *Interior Castle*, fourth mansion, chapter 2.

the period of prayer. We have been looking for happiness all our lives in the wrong places and now have suddenly found the direction in which it can be found. Naturally, we are going to want to prolong the experience as long as possible. As a result, some people are inclined to add more time to their prayer period on a regular basis. This may well be an inspiration of grace. However, they should not extend the time of formal prayer just because they are enjoying consolation. They no doubt have duties to fulfill of one kind or another, and enjoying long periods of deep recollection is not meant to replace them. At the same time, they may need to experience for a while the great goodness and tenderness of God because of feelings of self-rejection—especially if genuine affection from family and acquaintances was minimal or missing in early childhood. The prayer of quiet may go on for years.

The Prayer of Union

At some point, the Spirit may grasp the will even tighter. The psychological experience that follows from this union of wills is that the imagination and memory are both temporarily suspended by the divine action. God, so to speak, opens his heart to us and, to make sure that we don't miss the point or fail to receive the fullness of his grace, puts to rest the mental obstacles in us by suspending the reflective faculties for a few moments or longer. We are then ready to take all the pleasures of this world and drop them in the wastebasket. Nothing can compare with the delights of the divine presence. This is the Prayer of Union in which the will is completely united with God and one is fully aware of it.

The Prayer of Full Union

Should God tighten his grip even more, one enters the Prayer of Full Union. This grace takes away all self-reflection. One is not even aware that one is in this state until it is over. Afterwards, one knows that one has been in a spiritual place that was marvelous. Not only does the Spirit suspend the ordinary reflective faculties, but even suspends the sense of an individual self. At least for the moment, one loses all interest in what it has ever done or of what becomes of it. According to St. Teresa, the Prayer of Full Union does not last long. She writes that she would be surprised if it lasted more than half an hour. However, it may be repeated at various levels of intensity in the same period of prayer.

On the other hand, it may happen only once or twice in one's lifetime. It may also subside after a period of great frequency and then stop altogether. The likelihood for most contemplatives is that the Prayer of Quiet will become their habitual state of prayer. Once one has gotten used to it, one does not notice its sweetness and consolation so much, and the period of prayer can seem to be rather dry. It remains however, refreshing, nourishing, and necessary for the continued growth of the contemplative state and its transforming effects.

The Grace of Transforming Union

Compared to the Transforming Union, particular graces, however sublime and exalting, are only partial communications of God. They have great value in orienting us toward the Transforming Union. They also support our journey into the state of no-thing-ness, where even our attachment to our own identity is relinquished. One sign of Transforming Union is to manifest God's goodness and tenderness in whatever the "now moment" contains or seems to require. It is to do what God wants us to do and to react as God wants us to react in the present moment.

The Transforming Union tends to conceal the enormous work of grace that is going on in us. We are finally learning what it means for the Father to see in secret and what it means for us to pray in secret. God's action is continuously manifesting itself in us. Our call is primarily to respond to the inspirations of grace as far as we can perceive them and to allow ourselves to be moved by the Spirit through the Fruits and the Seven Gifts of the Spirit, the empirical evidence, so to speak, that we are "in Christ Jesus" (Romans 8:1). We are a kind of fifth Gospel (not canonical, of course), but nonetheless a witness not only to the teaching of Jesus, but to the *experience* that Jesus had of the Father as *Abba*, the God of unconditional Love.

As the false self diminishes the True Self builds a new self which Paul calls "the new creation." He describes it thus:

I live no longer I, but Christ lives in me (Galatians 2:20).

We still have a life, but it is no longer the life of the false self.

Unity

But the state of divine union still involves two people. Their oneness is so complete that they each want to pour themselves into the other and become the other. Yet beyond the Transforming Union there is a further development revealed by the mystery of the Ascension in which even the Transforming Union is transcended. According to the Beguines (a thirteenth-century lay movement), especially Hadewijch of Antwerp and Marguerite Porete, one is united to God in the unity of the Holy Spirit in the same way that the Father and the Son are united. This perfect oneness seems to be referred to in Jesus' prayer at the Last Supper,

That they may all be one, as you, Father, are in me and I am in you, that they also may be one in us. . . . I have given them the glory you gave me, so that they may be one as we are one, I in them and you in me, that they may be brought to perfection as one, that the world may know that you sent me, and that you love them even as you love me (John 17:20–23).

CHAPTER FIFTEEN

A Response to the Signs of the Times

Centering Prayer is a kind of distillation of monastic prayer, but without the special environment of a monastery. With the long tradition of monastic spirituality behind them, monks in general do not feel that they need a method beyond what is contained in the Rule of St. Benedict, which they follow. Their fundamental contemplative practice is *Lectio Divina*, which might be paraphrased as "reading the book believed to be divinely inspired."

Monastics are accustomed to moving toward contemplation through the practice of prayerful listening to the word of God in scripture with an ever-deepening attitude of attentiveness.

About two thirds of the way through the twentieth century, there was a movement among spiritual teachers of major world religions to come to the United States and to present their respective methods of. meditation (Contemplative Prayer in Christian terminology). These spiritual masters proclaimed their teaching in the form of methods that were carefully worked out, noteworthy for their psychological wisdom, and based on the experience of centuries of dedicated people who had both enjoyed the fruits of their varied forms of meditation and endured its difficulties.

The Centering Prayer Movement

At the monastery of St. Joseph's Abbey, Spencer, Massachusetts, where I was Abbot from 1961 to 1981, a number of young people who had attended sessions with the spiritual masters of other traditions came from time to time to check us out. The spiritual teachings communicated to them by Eastern teachers were usually accompanied by a concrete method. It was as if these students were saying to us: "Here is the method we learned in this particular Eastern spiritual tradition. Where is yours?" Christian tradition at that time had virtually no answer to this question.

It occurred to me that we monks might be able to put the essence of the Christian contemplative tradition into a specific method, too. The monastic lifestyle itself is a method in the broad sense of a rule of life, but it is not designed for the specific psycho-spiritual needs of individual monks and nuns. It seemed that, having studied the Christian contemplative tradition deeply for many years and having tried to live it, we might do something to make it more accessible and better understood by people of our time.

One of the purposes of the Second Vatican Council was to articulate the Roman Catholic tradition in terms that were better adapted to modern times. Much progress was accomplished on the level of liturgical and theological reform. By presenting the contemplative tradition in the form of a method, we hoped to transmit to people living in the world the healing and transforming values of the Christian contemplative heritage that we had learned and were living in the monastery.

Centering Prayer is a distillation of the essence of the Egyptian monastic experience of the third and fourth centuries translated to the West by John Cassian and maintained primarily in the West through the Rule of St. Benedict. The name Centering Prayer was suggested in an early retreat given to priests and religious. At that time we expected that our work would be to train interested priests and religious in how to teach the method. Since it was their vocation to minister to people in the world, we hoped that they would share it with the Christian community, once they had practiced it for a while and learned how to present it to others in an effective manner.

In actual fact, it wasn't long before we discovered that many laypersons were just as interested in acquiring a deeper knowledge of the Christian spiritual life as priests and religious. They had intuitively perceived that it was present somewhere, even though hard to find. With this in mind, a series of Centering Prayer retreats were presented at the guesthouse at the Spencer monastery. These were attended at first by priests, then by religious, and finally by laypersons.

The Christian contemplative tradition had long been forgotten in Christian circles—put on the shelf or at best reserved for monks and nuns in cloisters. It was not available to the rank and file of parishioners or students in Catholic schools and seminaries. The Church was in a spiritual desert and for various historical and other reasons had remained there for centuries. I personally encountered this problem when I was looking for a place to go to cultivate Contemplative Prayer as a young man. No one I consulted thought it existed outside of a monastery or convent.

It was poignant to see sincere people completely unaware of their own Christian contemplative heritage going to India and Southeast Asia, at great cost to themselves, to seek what they did not know was available at home. While for the most part they greatly profited from Eastern spiritual practices, the teachings sometimes created difficulties for their Christian faith.

It seemed to us that it was time for the Christian contemplative tradition to rise from the oblivion into which it had fallen. Even genuine Christian seekers believed that there was no contemplative practice in the Christian tradition comparable to what the Eastern religions provided. Based on my experience of Contemplative Prayer, I felt that the Christian religion should at least be represented in the marketplace as a path to transformation and union with God. My colleagues, Father William Meninger, Father Basil Pennington, and others agreed, and Father Meninger started offering Centering Prayer to retreatants in the Abbey guesthouse in 1975.

In the next few years it became clear that a lot of people were interested in learning about the Christian contemplative heritage. As they practiced the method of Centering Prayer on a twice daily basis many found significant benefits—among them, greater peace in everyday life and strength to meet its difficulties. Some stated that they could not have gotten through certain heavy trials that they came upon them, without their regular daily practice. Retreats that provided longer periods of Centering Prayer inspired some to want to share the method with others. It began to be taught in more and more places. The response justified our growing conviction that Centering Prayer spoke to an immense need in the broader Christian community and that it was a genuine movement of the Holy Spirit.

Once we were convinced that this was coming from the inspiration of the Spirit, our next concern was to figure out the best way to deliver the method and its immediate conceptual background. In that way, we believed people learning the method would have a better chance of tasting the experience of God and persevering in the practice.

The Establishment of Contemplative Outreach
At the end of 1984, a small group of practitioners estab-

lished a structure called Contemplative Outreach to serve as a spiritual network to transmit the method and to develop programs that responded to the needs of the growing movement. Besides fostering the practice of Centering Prayer and its immediate conceptual background, it was designed as a way to keep in touch with the membership of the network and to develop practices that would foster the contemplative dimension of the Gospel in everyday life. The leadership of the network made it a principle to listen to the experience of those who took up the prayer and to respond to needs as they arise with new programs and advanced training. Contemplative Outreach is now a multi-layered organization of persons who are experiencing the practice at different levels and need specific spiritual nourishment for the particular issues that arose at each level.

As this book has noted, Centering Prayer is a way of detailing the general formula that Jesus puts forward in Matthew 6:6. "If you want to pray, enter your inner room, close the door, and pray to your *Abba* (Father) in secret, and your *Abba* who sees in secret will reward you."

What is the reward? I suggest the meaning might be, God will take care of everything else. The whole thrust of the prayer is to turn the practitioner over to the inspirations of the Holy Spirit. As Paul teaches,

We don't know how to pray as we ought, but the Spirit itself intercedes with inexpressible groanings (Romans 8:26).

Groanings are not words, obviously, but manifestations of great desire and longing. The network seeks to
address that vast population of people touched by God
that transcends cultural, geographical, denominational,
and religious boundaries.[11]

The Three Purposes of Contemplative Outreach

In the book *Open Mind, Open Heart*, the three general
purposes for establishing the spiritual network of
Contemplative Outreach are listed.

The first is to renew the contemplative tradition of the
Roman Catholic Church. By the time of writing the book,
we had already been approached by people of other
denominations who were just as interested in the contemplative life and Centering Prayer as a practical way to pre-
pare oneself for it as the Roman Catholics we had encountered. Because of the extensive character of their interest,
we came to believe that this method was intended by God
for Christians across denominational boundaries.

The ancient apophatic tradition of Contemplative
Prayer, rooted in Jesus' teaching in Matthew 6:6, was
refined by the early Fathers of the Church and more particularly by the Fathers and Mothers of the desert of the
third and fourth centuries. It predates all heresies and
schisms and hence belongs to all Christians: Eastern

---

11. See Appendix I (p. 129) for the Vision Statement and Theological
Foundations of the Contemplative Outreach Network.

Orthodox, Anglicans, Protestants, and Evangelicals as well as Roman Catholics.

Our second purpose, accordingly, is to make the Christian Contemplative heritage available to the other Christian communities. We knew from our experience of praying together with people of different denominations that Centering Prayer bonds the participants in a way that transcends doctrinal differences, not in the sense of denying their importance, but by emphasizing the *experience* of the living Christ as our common bond of unity. We leave to each person to pursue, as his or her own conscience may dictate, the theological or doctrinal formation that they have received. Centering Prayer is not the time to think and reflect. We invite participants in the sacred circle to be still, motionless within and without, interiorly quiet and silent, and to experience what is deeper and more unifying than theological reflection. Actually, the presence of God within us is deeper than consciousness itself. It is this loving presence of God within each of us that Jesus identified as *Abba*. This is the endearing term for the Divine Mystery to which we open ourselves as we pray whether in private or together.

Obviously doctrinal discussions between the various denominations have to continue in order to seek unity at the theological level. Meanwhile, having found unity at a deeper level, it is our purpose to share equally with our Protestant brothers and sisters the whole of the apophatic tradition as we have received it.

The third purpose of Contemplative Outreach is to pre-
pare Christians for more profound interreligious dialogue. Not far from the Abbey at Spencer, Massachusetts,
is the Buddhist Insight Meditation Center. Many out-
standing Buddhist teachers who taught there in the 1970s
visited us to see what the Christian monastic scene might
be like. Perhaps one of the more significant interreligious
events at that time was the creation, at the instigation of
the Vatican Congregation for Interreligious Dialogue, of
an exchange of monks and nuns from the Benedictine,
Cistercian and Camaldolese orders to dialogue with
monks and nuns of the other world religions. This long-
term dialogue enabled people with extensive contemplative experience to share with each other what most helped
them in their respective spiritual traditions to advance in
the Spiritual Journey and to thus be inspired by each
other. We found some of these insights valuable in uncov-
ering certain depths of the Christian contemplative tradition through the emphasis that Eastern spiritual traditions
give to various aspects of their meditative practices. There
is much to be learned from interreligious dialogue to
enrich one's grasp of the spiritual journey in one's own
tradition. Until recently we were in almost total ignorance
of each other's profound wisdom teachings. We still have
a long way to go in order to grasp the advanced stages of
the major spiritual traditions of the world, especially how
these relate to the ultimate experience of God. But the
foundations are gradually being laid.

Can Centering Prayer Be Offered to People without Any Religion?

Through the three objectives outlined above, we hoped to contribute to raising the level of consciousness in the Christian community that Contemplative Prayer is available to everyone. The hunger for a deeper life of prayer and for closer union with God, right now, is immense and seems to exist all over the world.

This phenomenon has brought me to the conviction that there is a profound truth in Karl Rahner's teaching that nature itself is graced. Medieval theology sharply distinguished nature and grace. Roman Catholic teaching in recent centuries had almost come to see them as opposites. But if nature is in fact graced, everybody, even through sources other than religion, can taste the presence of God. God manifests himself through the rituals and spiritual disciplines of the various religions of the world, but God also draws people through the love of nature, science, the service of others, spiritual friendship, conjugal love, art, professional skills, work, play, silence, solitude and other ways that can elicit a sense of God's presence. We must not think to deprive God of his freedom or limit his activity to working only in relationship with religious beliefs and practices. One needs to remember the various covenants God made with members of the human family to which the Old Testament bears witness, e.g. God's covenants with Noah, Abraham, Moses, and Melchizedek. Presumably these are still in force. What prevents God from having covenants with individuals or communities without specific religious practices? According to the Prologue of John's Gospel, God enlightens everyone entering the world. In virtue of being born everyone is in relations to the Word.

The Prison Ministry

The experience of teaching Centering Prayer in prisons has reinforced my belief in the extent to which God is prepared to go in order to reach people wherever they are. When we first introduced Centering Prayer in prisons, we notice that most men on the yard were not interested in coming to the chapel for religious services. They were beyond the reach of representatives of any religion. They were allergic to words like God, faith, forgiveness, and religion. They disliked the whole idea of religion and religious attitudes.

In Folsom State Prison in Represa, California, several of the inmates found the book *Open Mind, Open Heart* and started practicing Centering Prayer on their own. They asked for a representative of Contemplative Outreach to come in and give them a formal introductory workshop in Centering Prayer. The group came to be known as the Contemplative Fellowship. It met one night a week (provided there wasn't a lockdown), spent twenty minutes in silence and shared their experience. A core group took charge of teaching their fellow inmates how to do Centering Prayer. When other inmates saw changes for the better in the lives of these prisoners, some of them began to get interested in what they were doing to effect these changes. And as they began to attend the meetings and to experience silence themselves, they too began to change. They became less aggressive, angry, discouraged, more cheerful and considerate. Some even began to attend church services.

God's determination to save everyone (1 Timothy 2:4) is not just to save people in general, but to transform each member of the human family in their inmost being and to bring them to the fullness of divine life and love. God seems to want us to extend every possible means in his power to touch people just where they are. If they have no religion at all, the Divine Presence will try to reach them by some other means. This has been done with amazing results in the program called the Twelve Steps of Alcoholics Anonymous. In that program, now adapted to all kinds of addictive behavior, the principal requirement is to believe in a Higher Power, which can be anything higher than we experience ourselves to be.

Letting go of the entrenched self-centeredness of the ego by regular practices of silence gives God an opening, and with that opening the image of God in our inmost being begins to reassert itself. Since it can never be lost, it can always be reawakened. My conclusion is that we need to expand our ideas of God's mercy, which reaches out much farther than we can possibly imagine. Actually, no one can ever come to the end of it.

As we extend the availability of Centering Prayer to people, we must also extend its effects to the whole of creation, especially to this planet—to the animals, plants, minerals, earth, air, and water—not forgetting the subatomic world and all the galaxies. We have to embrace with admiration and love all of God's creation, however vast and however infinitesimal. Everything is interrelated and interdependent because everything has the same Source.

Here is the text that summarizes the vision of Contemplative Outreach:

> Contemplative Outreach is a spiritual network of individuals and small faith communities committed to living the contemplative dimension of the Gospel in everyday life through the practice of Centering Prayer. The contemplative dimension of the Gospel manifests itself in an ever-deepening union with the living Christ and the practical caring for others that flows from that relationship.
>
> Our purpose is to share the method of Centering Prayer and its immediate conceptual background. We also encourage the practice of *Lectio Divina*, particularly its movement into Contemplative Prayer, which a regular and established practice of Centering Prayer facilitates.
>
> We identify with the Christian contemplative heritage. While we are formed by our respective

denominations, we are united in our common search for God and the experience of the living Christ through Centering Prayer. We affirm our solidarity with the contemplative dimension of other religions and sacred traditions, with the needs and rights of the whole human family, and with all creation.

Paul writes that at some point in time or after its completion "God will be all in all" (1 Corinthians 15:28). Since God is love, God's unconditional love will also be all in all. This invincible hope inspires the effort to offer to everyone a path to union with the oneness and infinite diversity of *That Which Is*.

Pure Prayer

The method of prayer that Centering Prayer tries to foster is the one John Cassian and Rule of St. Benedict call "Pure Prayer." This method of "pure prayer," expressed in Cassian's *Conferences, no. 9*, is much further developed in later tradition, especially in *The Cloud of Unknowing*, by the anonymous fourteenth-century author as well as by St. John of the Cross in the sixteenth century (cf. *The Living Flame of Love*, stanza iii, 26–59). The Centering Prayer method is a synthesis of these and other sources drawn from the Christian Contemplative Heritage.

In *Conference 9* of the *Conferences of Cassian*[12] Abba Issac is quoted as saying,

> We need to be especially careful to follow the Gospel precepts which instruct us to go into our

---

12. John Cassian, *Conferences*, translated by Colm Luibheid, Classics of Christian Spirituality, Paulist Press, 1985.

room and shut the door so that we may pray to out Father (Matthew 6:6) and this is how we can do it.

We pray in our room whenever we withdraw our hearts completely from the tumult and the noise of our thoughts and our worries, and when secretly and intimately we offer our prayers to the Lord.

We pray in secret when in our hearts alone and in our recollected spirits, we address God and reveal our wishes only to Him and in such a way that the hostile powers themselves have no inkling of their nature. Hence we must pray in utter silence . . . to insure that the thrust of our pleading be hidden from our enemies who are especially lying in wait to attack us during our prayers. In this way we shall fulfill the command, "Keep your mouth shut from the one who sleeps on your breast" (Micah 7:5).

The Method of Centering Prayer

The Prayer of Consent
"Be still and know that I am God." (Psalm 46:10)

Contemplative Prayer
We may think of prayer as thoughts or feelings expressed in words, but this is only one expression. In the Christian tradition, Contemplative Prayer is considered to be the pure gift of God. It is the opening of mind and heart—our whole being—to God, the Ultimate Mystery, beyond thoughts, words, and emotions. Through grace we open our awareness to God who we know by faith is within us, closer than breathing, closer than thinking, closer than choosing—closer than consciousness itself.

Centering Prayer
Centering Prayer is a method designed to facilitate the development of Contemplative Prayer by preparing our faculties to receive this gift. It is an attempt to present the

teaching of earlier times in an updated form. Centering Prayer is not meant to replace other kinds of prayer: rather it casts a new light and depth of meaning on them. It is at the same time a relationship with God and a discipline to foster that relationship. This method of prayer is a movement beyond conversation with Christ to communion with Him.

Theological Background

The source of Centering Prayer, as in all methods leading to Christian Contemplative Prayer, is the indwelling Trinity: Father, Son and Holy Spirit. The focus of Centering Prayer is the deepening of our relationship with the living Christ. It tends to build communities of faith and bond the members together in mutual friendship and love.

Listening to the Word of God in Scripture

Listening to the word of God in Scripture (*Lectio Divina*) is a traditional way of cultivating friendship with Christ. It is a way of listening to the texts of Scripture as if we were in conversation with Christ and he was suggesting the topics of conversation. The daily encounter with Christ and reflection on his word leads beyond mere acquaintanceship to an attitude of friendship, trust, and love. Conversation simplifies and gives way to communing. Gregory the Great (sixth century), summarizing the Christian contemplative tradition, expressed it as "resting in God." This was the classical meaning of Contemplative Prayer in the Christian tradition for the first sixteen centuries.

Wisdom Saying of Jesus

Centering Prayer is based on the wisdom saying of Jesus in the Sermon on the Mount:

> If you want to pray, enter your inner room, close the door, and pray to your Father in secret, and your Father who sees in secret will reward you (Matthew 6:6).

It is also inspired by writings of major contributors to the Christian contemplative heritage, including John Cassian, the anonymous author of *The Cloud of Unknowing*, Francis de Sales, Teresa of Avila, John of the Cross, Thérèse of Lisieux, and Thomas Merton.

The Guidelines

1. Choose a sacred word as the symbol of your intention to consent to God's presence and action within.
2. Sitting comfortably and with eyes closed, settle briefly and silently introduce the sacred word as the symbol of your consent to God's presence and action within.
3. When engaged with your thoughts,* return ever so gently to the sacred word.

4. At the end of the prayer period, remain in silence with eyes closed for a couple of minutes.

Centering Prayer Guidelines
I. Choose a sacred word as the symbol of your intention to consent to God's presence and action within. (cf. *Open Mind, Open Heart,* Thomas Keating, chapter 5).

1. The sacred word expresses our intention to consent to God's presence and action within.
2. The sacred word is chosen during a brief period of prayer asking the Holy Spirit to inspire us with one that is especially suitable for us.
   a. Examples: God, Jesus, *Abba*, Father, Mother, Mary, Amen.
   b. Other possibilities: Love, Peace, Listen, Mercy,Let Go, Silence, Faith, Trust, Yes.
3. Instead of a sacred word, a simple inward glance toward the Divine Presence or noticing one's breath may be more suitable for some persons. *The same guidelines apply to these symbols as to the sacred word.*
4. The sacred word is sacred not because of its inherent meaning but because of the meaning we give it as the expression of our intention and consent.
5. Having chosen a sacred word, we do not change it

---

*Thoughts include body sensations, feelings, images, concepts, and reflections.

during the prayer period because that would be to start thinking again.

II. *Sitting comfortably and with eyes closed, settle briefly and silently introduce the sacred word as the symbol of your consent to God's presence and action within.*

1. "Sitting comfortably" means relatively comfortably, so as not to encourage sleep during the time of prayer.

2. Whatever sitting position we choose, we keep our back straight.

3. We close our eyes as a symbol of letting go of what is going on around and within us.

4. We introduce the sacred word inwardly, as gently as laying a feather on a piece of absorbent cotton.

5. Should we fall asleep, upon awakening we continue the prayer.

III. *When engaged with your thoughts, return ever-so-gently to the sacred word.*

1. "Thoughts" is an umbrella term for every perception, including body sensations, sense perceptions, feelings, images, memories, reflections, concepts, commentaries, and spiritual experiences.

2. "Thoughts" are inevitable, integral and a normal part of Centering Prayer.

3. By "returning ever so gently to the sacred word," a minimum of effort is indicated. This is the only

activity we initiate during the time of Centering Prayer.

4. During the course of Centering Prayer, the sacred word may become vague or even disappear.

IV. At the end of the prayer period, remain in silence with eyes closed for a couple of minutes.

1. The additional two minutes enables us to bring the atmosphere of silence into everyday life.

2. If this prayer is done in a group, the leader may slowly recite a prayer such as the Lord's Prayer while the others listen.

Practical Points

1. The minimum time for this prayer is twenty minutes. Two periods are recommended each day, one first thing in the morning and one in the afternoon or early evening. With practice, the time may be extended to thirty minutes or longer.

2. The end of the prayer period can be indicated by a timer, provided it does not have an audible tick or loud sound when it goes off.

3. Possible physical symptoms during the prayer:

   a. We may notice slight pains, itches, or twitches in various parts of the body or a generalized sense of restlessness. These are usually due to the untying of emotional knots in the body.

   b. We may notice heaviness or lightness in our

extremities. This is usually due to a deep level of spiritual attentiveness.

c. In either case, we pay no attention, or we allow the mind to rest briefly in the sensation, and then return to the sacred word.

4. The principal fruits of the prayer are experienced in daily life and not during the prayer period.

5. Centering Prayer familiarizes us with the language of God, which is silence.

Points for Further Development

1. During the prayer period, various kinds of thoughts may arise. (cf. *Open Mind, Open Heart*, chapters 6–10.)

   a. Ordinary wanderings of the imagination or memory.

   b. Thoughts and feelings that give rise to attractions or aversions.

   c. Insights and psychological breakthroughs.

   d. Self-reflections such as, "How am I doing?" or, "This peace is just great!"

   e. Thoughts and feelings that arise from the unloading of the unconscious.

   When engaged with such thoughts, return ever so gently to your sacred word.

2. During this prayer we avoid analyzing our experience, harboring expectations, or aiming at some specific goal such as:

    a. Repeating the sacred word continuously.

    b. Having no thoughts.

    c. Making the mind a blank.

    d. Feeling peaceful or consoled.

    e. Achieving a spiritual experience.

Ways to Deepen Our Relationship with God

1. Practice two twenty- to thirty-minute periods of Centering Prayer daily.

2. Listen to the Word of God in Scripture and study *Open Mind, Open Heart.*

3. Select one or two of the specific practices for everyday life as suggested in *Open Mind, Open Heart,* chapter 12.

4. Join a weekly Centering Prayer Group.

    a. It encourages the members of the group to persevere in their individual practices.

    b. It provides an opportunity for further input on a regular basis through tapes, readings, and discussion.

    c. It offers an opportunity to support and share the spiritual journey.

What Centering Prayer Is and Is Not

- It is not a technique but a way of cultivating God's friendship.

- It is not a relaxation exercise but it may be refreshing.

- It is not a form of self-hypnosis but a way to quiet the mind while maintaining its alertness.
- It is not a charismatic gift but a path of transformation.
- It is not a para-psychological experience but an exercise of faith, hope, and selfless love.
- It is not limited to the "felt" presence of God but is rather a deepening of faith in God's abiding presence.
- It is not reflective or spontaneous prayer, but simply resting in God.

For Information and Resources Contact:

Contemplative Outreach Ltd.

10 Park Place

PO Box 737

Butler, NJ 07405

Tel: (973) 838-3384 / Fax: (973) 492-5795

Email: office@coutreach.org

Website: www.contemplativeoutreach.org

Visit our website at www.contemplativeoutreach.org for events, retreats, articles, and the online bookstore.